Yarrow

Herb of the Year™ 2024

International Herb Association
Compiled and edited by Kathleen Connole

IHA HERB OF THE YEAR™

Each year the International Herb Association chooses an **Herb of the Year™** to highlight. The Horticulture Committee evaluates possible choices based on their being outstanding in at least two of the three major categories: culinary, medicinal, and ornamental. Herbal organizations around the world work together with us to educate the public throughout the year.

Herb of the Year™ books are published annually by the

International Herb Association
P.O. Box 5667 Jacksonville, Florida 32247-5667
www.iherb.org

This book is intended as an informational guide. The remedies, approaches, and techniques described herein are meant to supplement, and not to be a substitute for professional medical care or treatment; please consult your health care provider.

The International Herb Association is a professional trade organization providing education, service, and development for members engaged in all aspects of the herbal industry.

ISBN: 979-8-9878959-2-4

Uniting Herb Professionals for Growth
Through Promotion and Education

The International Herb Association has some of the most dedicated volunteers who keep the organization afloat, giving their time and talents to ensure that IHA continues to share herbal knowledge and connect those in the profession of herbs. We are deeply indebted to the IHA Board of Directors, the IHA Foundation members, and our webmaster. Thanks for all that you do and for caring enough to move us forward!

Acknowledgments

When I first agreed to edit *Yarrow Herb of the Year™ 2024,* I will admit that I wondered why this herb had been chosen. Even though it is a common wildflower and garden favorite, and most of us know how it got the Latin name *Achillea,* I had never heard of any uses except that the leaves truly do stop bleeding, that it attracts pollinators and is beautiful in fresh or dried flower arrangements. The study of yarrow reveals that it has been used medicinally for thousands of years for a wide range of health problems.

Susan Belsinger describes the botany of *Achillea* and is most helpful in explaining how to tell yarrow from some similar looking plants. Tina Marie Wilcox writes of her experiences growing and using yarrow in the Ozarks, including starting wild (white-blooming) yarrow from seed. Yarrow is a favorite flower for pollinators, and Diann Nance discovers which butterfly uses it as a host plant. Marge Powell has colorful yarrow cultivars growing in her garden which she compares to wild yarrow in an interesting experiment. Gert Coleman has found yarrow references in poetry, mythology, and folklore, and some promising uses beyond the physical. Rosemary Roman Davis gives us some little-known history of yarrow, a bit of folklore, and includes her favorite yarrow recipes.

Susan Belsinger and Pat Kenny share their long history with the *I Ching* and yarrow's role in this ancient practice.

As an herb for flavor, yarrow presents quite the challenge. Culinary artists Pat Crocker and Karen England rise to the occasion with recipes for unique dishes, condiments, and beverages.

Janice Cox has provided lovely recipes using yarrow for health and beauty.

Achillea is best known in the herbal world for its use as a remedy for multiple conditions. Daniel Gagnon presents detailed explanations of yarrow's beneficial properties and relevant studies of medicinal uses. Carol Little shares her practical experience using yarrow as medicine and provides us with recipes. Yarrow essential oil is a powerful remedy that Dorene Petersen has much experience with; she analyzes its unique composition and gives us careful advice on its use.

Finally, IHA Horticulture Committee Chair, Chuck Voigt, gives us his perspective on the history of the Herb of the Year™ program and how *Achillea* came to be the 2024 selection.

I am forever indebted to Gert Coleman and Susan Belsinger for their expert editorial skills as second readers. They are patient teachers, and I continue to be humbled at how much there is yet to learn. Karen Kalergis was very helpful as a second reader of the in-depth scientific articles on the medicinal uses of yarrow.

A great variety of yarrow photographs have been provided by Susan Belsinger, Gert Coleman, Heather Cohen, Janice Cox, Pat Crocker, Karen England, Pat Kenny, Dorene Petersen, Marge Powell, and Tina Marie Wilcox. We sincerely appreciate our talented illustrators, Susan Belsinger, Pat Kenny, Alicia Mann, Gail Wood Miller, and Skye Suter.

It is wonderful to again have the collaboration between Susan Belsinger and Heather Cohen on the beautiful Yarrow cover design. We are delighted to have Heather as our professional layout person. Her expertise and talent enable us to produce the book in just the way that we envision it.

I would like to thank the IHA Board and Foundation for their support and encouragement as we carry on the Herb of the Year tradition for this, its 30th year. I continue to be amazed and enlightened!

I owe many thanks to my family for their tolerance and understanding as I devote my time and attention to this third year as HOY editor. They are getting to learn along with me, as we discover the benefits of another "herb," going way beyond the common perception of herbs as parsley, sage, rosemary, and thyme.

~Kathleen Connole, Editor

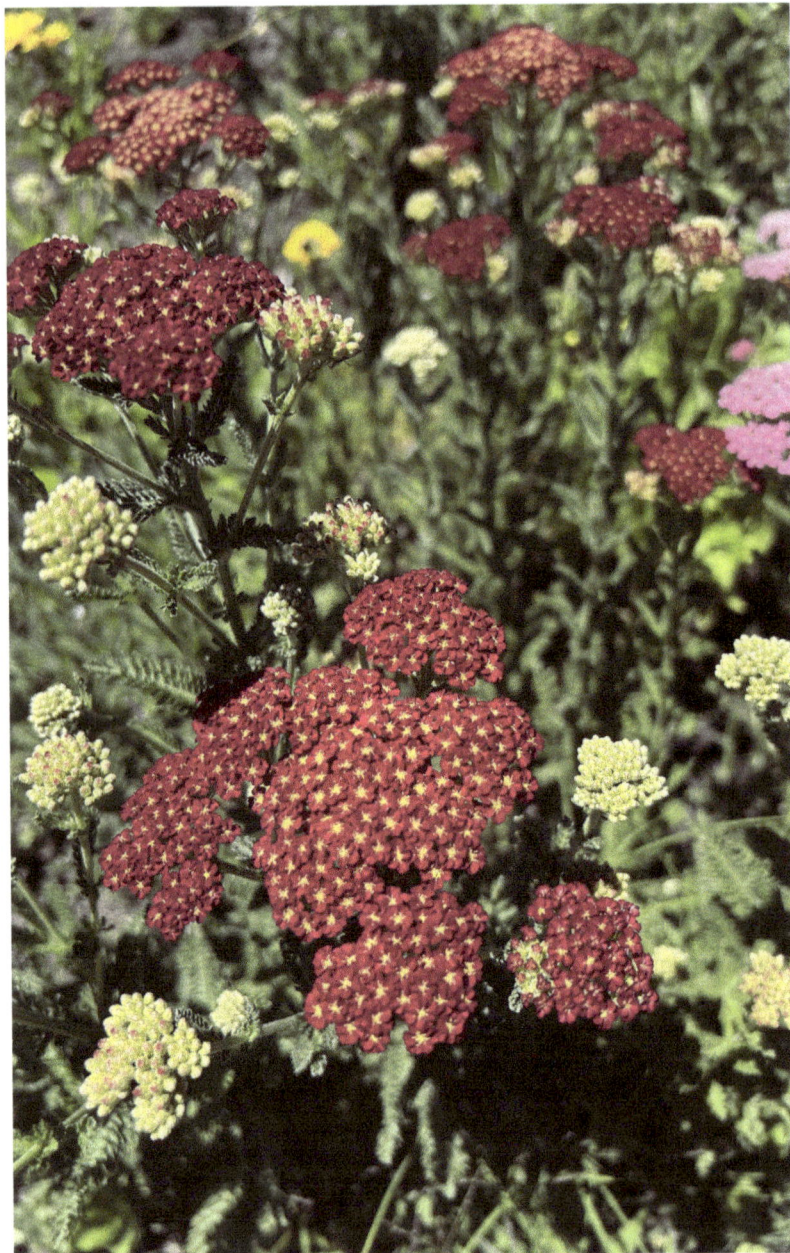

Brilliant red 'Paprika' yarrow cultivar is outstanding in the garden and attracts many pollinators, even hummingbirds. *Janice Cox*

Table of Contents

Yarrow Recipes

Medicinal Uses of Yarrow

Knowing and Growing Yarrow

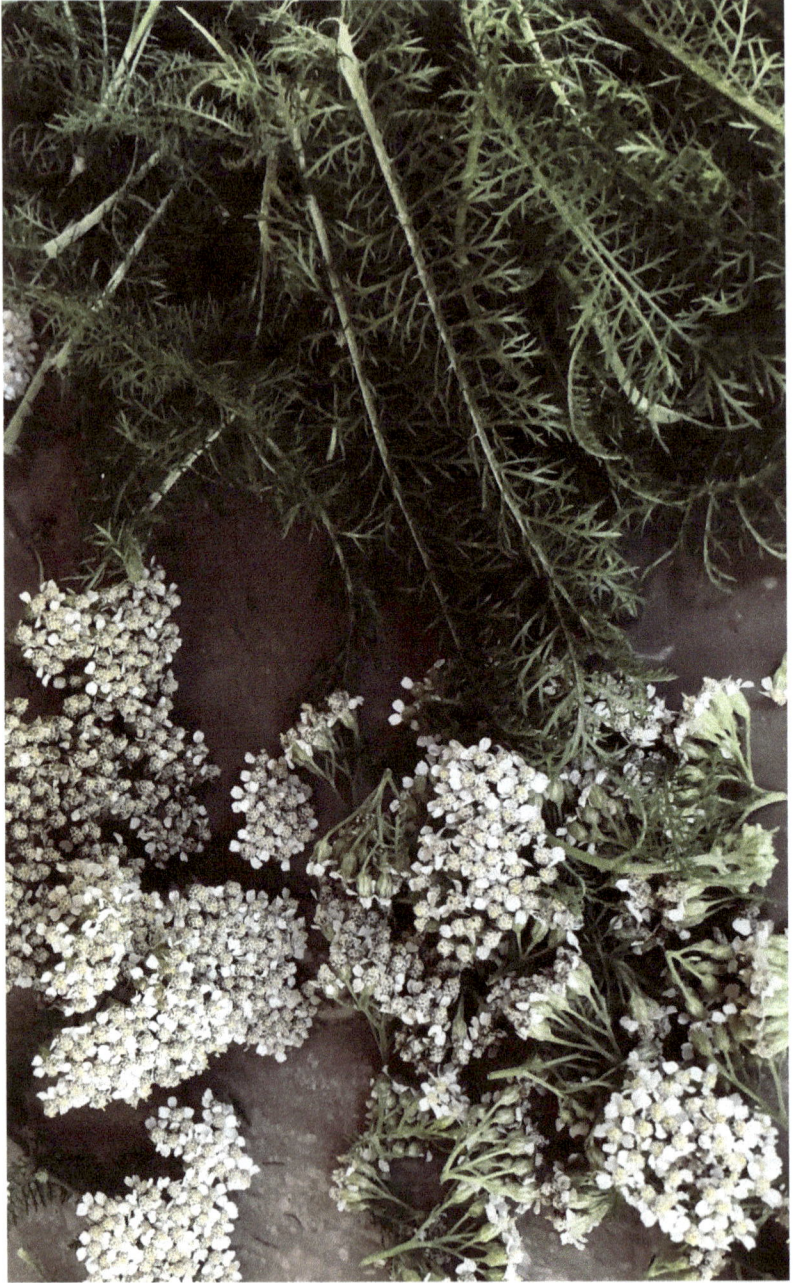

Feathery leaves and white-flowered corymbs are two distinguishing traits of *Achillea millefolium. Susan Belsinger*

Knowing Yarrow

Susan Belsinger

I've known yarrow for over 50 years. Besides using the stalks for throwing the *I Ching* oracle, my first real acquaintance with *Achillea millefolium* was preparing a tisane from the leaves. I did this because it was recommended for relief of menstrual cramps. At that time in life, it was probably the most bitter thing that I had ever tasted. I do believe it may have helped with the cramps, though the ingesting of it was not very pleasant for a young adult having grown up in a non-bitter household full of sweet tooths, and not knowing or using herbal remedies.

Now, it is a plant grown in my garden and wild on the land and its dried flowers and leaves, powder, tincture and honey are always in my apothecary. It is important to harvest the flowers at just the right time or they will turn brown when dried. I keep an eye on the flowers as they bud up and cut the stems near the base (which should grow and provide another chance to flower during the season) just as the flowers open. If you wait until the whole flower head is open, they might turn brown while drying and they certainly will if left on the plant. My dried hanging bundles from this summer's harvest are still hanging and they are cream in color, two months or so later. I need to comminute them and put them in a jar for storage—at the ready for an herbal infusion when needed—or I might get around to making a yarrow bitters.

If you don't grow yarrow, it may very well be in your neighborhood growing wild in fields or meadows, even in vacant lots, waste places and along the roadsides—where the earth has been disturbed. Remember that we don't harvest on others' land without permission and certainly not directly from a roadside where there is automotive pollution. This "wild" yarrow has white flowers, sometimes with a pinkish tinge, feathery green leaves and reaches a height of 18 to 36 inches. Queen Anne's lace (*Daucus carota*) is a plant most often mistaken for yarrow that grows in similar areas and looks like yarrow from a distance, though side-by-side it is easy to distinguish the difference in the two plants (see photos on following page).

Yarrow flowers (left) are composed of corymbs while Queen Anne's lace (right) has umbels. *Susan Belsinger*

I will also mention one other plant here that can be mistaken for yarrow and that is poison hemlock (*Conium maculatum*), which is very toxic! In her article "Poison Hemlock: How to Identify and Potential Look-alikes," Colleen Codekas warns that "Mature poison hemlock plants are three to four times larger than yarrow and poison hemlock stems are hairless, hollow, and almost always have distinctive purplish-red splotching or streaking on them, especially towards the base of the plant" (www.growforagecookferment. com/poison-hemlock/).

Yarrow corymbs. *Vintage illustration, Public Domain*

Let's take a moment to talk about the plant botany here.

Achillea millefolium is in the dicotyledon class of flowering plants, aster subclass and aster order (Asterales). According to Thomas Elpel, in his excellent book *Botany in a Day*, yarrow belongs to the "Camomile Tribe," the distinguishing characteristics being that they are highly aromatic, and the bracts around the flower base are "scarious" meaning dry, thin and translucent. Inflorescences on these naturalized, perennial plants are made up of corymbs.

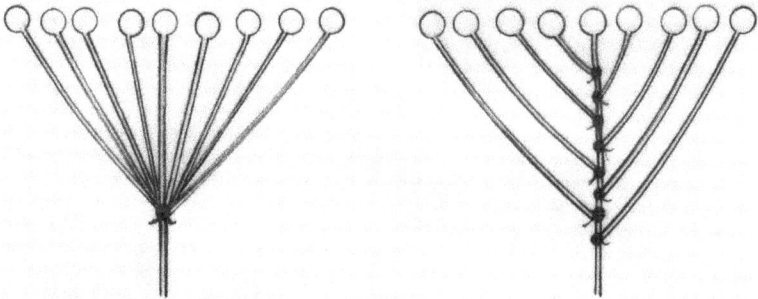

Umbel on left, corymb on right. Drawing by *Pat Kenny.*

Corymbs—A short, broad, flat-topped or slightly convex flower cluster with the inflorescence having the youngest flowers at the end of main axis. The pedicels of the lower flowers are longer than those of the upper flowers so that the inflorescence has a flat-topped look. Flowers in a corymb structure can be parallel or alternate, and the shape convex or flat; sometimes giving a superficial resemblance towards an umbel. Examples: yarrow, hawthorn, rowan, shepherd's purse, garlic mustard and yerba maté.

Umbels—A flower cluster, usually rounded, though sometimes the inflorescence is flat-topped with all the pedicels arising from a common point, sort of like umbrella ribs. (Can include simple and compound umbels.) Examples: Queen Anne's lace, carrot, dill, fennel, parsley and hemlock.

Cymes—A broad, somewhat flat-topped inflorescence in which the central flowers open first, followed by the peripheral flowers; a cyme can be compressed so that it looks like an umbel. (Can include simple, compound and scorpioid cymes.) Examples: elderberry, wild geranium, wood anemone and buttercup.

Close-up of yarrow flowers. *Susan Belsinger*

In her plant study, Jane Ellen Blossom (www.flowersociety.org/yarrow_plant_study.htm) describes the inflorescence in detail: "The bloom of the White Yarrow is a compact cluster of tiny white flowers with yellow centers. It appears there are approximately 5 to 6 white petals per tiny flower … sometimes one petal overlapping another. The umbrella-like, dense clusters of white flowers are flat-topped, and range in circumference between 1 and 6 inches on the plants I am viewing. Without a magnifying glass, it appears that there are tiny red-orange stamens sprouting up from the yellow centers. Upon closer observation, I notice each individual white flower petal is creased with several indented length-wise lines, and the outside tip of the petal reflects several notches giving it a slightly rippled effect."

Here's an apt description of yarrow's foliage by blogger Suzan Ferreira: "This erect perennial herb boasts beautiful, lovely fernlike foliage which is covered with 'hairs' creating a wooly-like silky texture." Leaves on the stem are alternate and have a lot of space between them closer to the base of the stem, and are closer together and much smaller in size as they come up the stem toward the bloom. Tiny top leaves might only be an inch long, while feathery leaves at the bottom can be six or eight inches in length. Each leaf has multitudes of tiny leaflets which gives the appearance of soft green feathers.

Stems become very woody at the end of the season in order to hold the plants upright. Some of the hybridized, ornamental yarrows can be woody-stemmed

Each *Achillea* leaf has a multitude of tiny leaflets, which gives them a feathery appearance. *Susan Belsinger*

and get up to 5 or 6 feet tall, especially the yellow ones which are quite hardy. The paprika, red, pink and burgundy varieties do not get nearly as tall; however their flowers sure are pretty.

All parts of the yarrow plant are useful: flowers, leaves, stems and roots. Supposedly, the plants are best harvested for potency in spring and summer, though I harvest them whenever I can. The flowers are higher in aromatic oils, while the leaves have more tannins. The common white yarrow has more medicinal virtues than the ornamental yarrows.

If you don't know yarrow very well, now is the time to get to know her better—here's to growing and knowing *Achillea millefolium*!

References

Bown, Deni. *The Herb Society of America Encyclopedia of Herbs & Their Uses*. Dorling Kindersley, 1995.

Elpel, Thomas. *Botany in a Day*, 4th Edition. Hops Press, 2000.

Els, David, ed. *The National Gardening Association Dictionary of Horticulture*. Penguin Books, 1994.

https://www.flowersociety.org/yarrow_plant_study.htm. Accessed 7/21/23.

https://www.waynesword.net/terminf1.htm. Accessed 7/21/23.

https://www.itsmysustainablelife.com/yarrow-its-many-uses. Accessed 8/13/23.

https://www.growforagecookferment.com/foraging-for-yarrow. Accessed 8/12/23.

https://www.growforagecookferment.com/poison-hemlock. Accessed 8/12/23.

https://scholarship.richmond.edu/cgi/viewcontent. cgi?article=1209&context=biology-faculty-publications. Accessed 8/12/23

https://en.wikipedia.org/wiki/Corymb. Accessed 10/28/23.

https://en.wikipedia.org/wiki/Umbel. Accessed 10/28/23.

https://en.wikipedia.org/wiki/Inflorescence. Accessed 10/28/23.

Susan Belsinger lives an herbal life—she teaches, lectures, and writes about herbs, gardening, and cooking—is a food writer, editor and photographer who has authored and edited over 25 books and hundreds of articles. She is celebrating her most recent book, *the perfect bite: focus on flavor*.

Susan is a member of the International Herb Association, the Herb Society of America and was Honorary President of the HSA for the 2018 to 2020 term. Check out her video series "Gathering and Preserving the Herbal Bounty" for HSA's online education: https://www.herbsociety.org/portal-log-in-page/on-line-education.html.

Susan delights in learning, whether it is about a person, place, plant, thing, or each new Herb of the Year: doing research, growing the specimens, botanizing, taking photos, creating recipes, sharing her findings and celebrating the plants.

www.susanbelsinger.com
https://www.instagram.com/cookinwithherbs/
https://www.facebook.com/susan.belsinger
https://www.facebook.com/CreativeHerbalHome

Dried yarrow leaves and flowers are essential to the apothecary. *Susan Belsinger*

Yarrow's elusive
scent faintly evokes grasses
waving in sunshine.

Gert Coleman

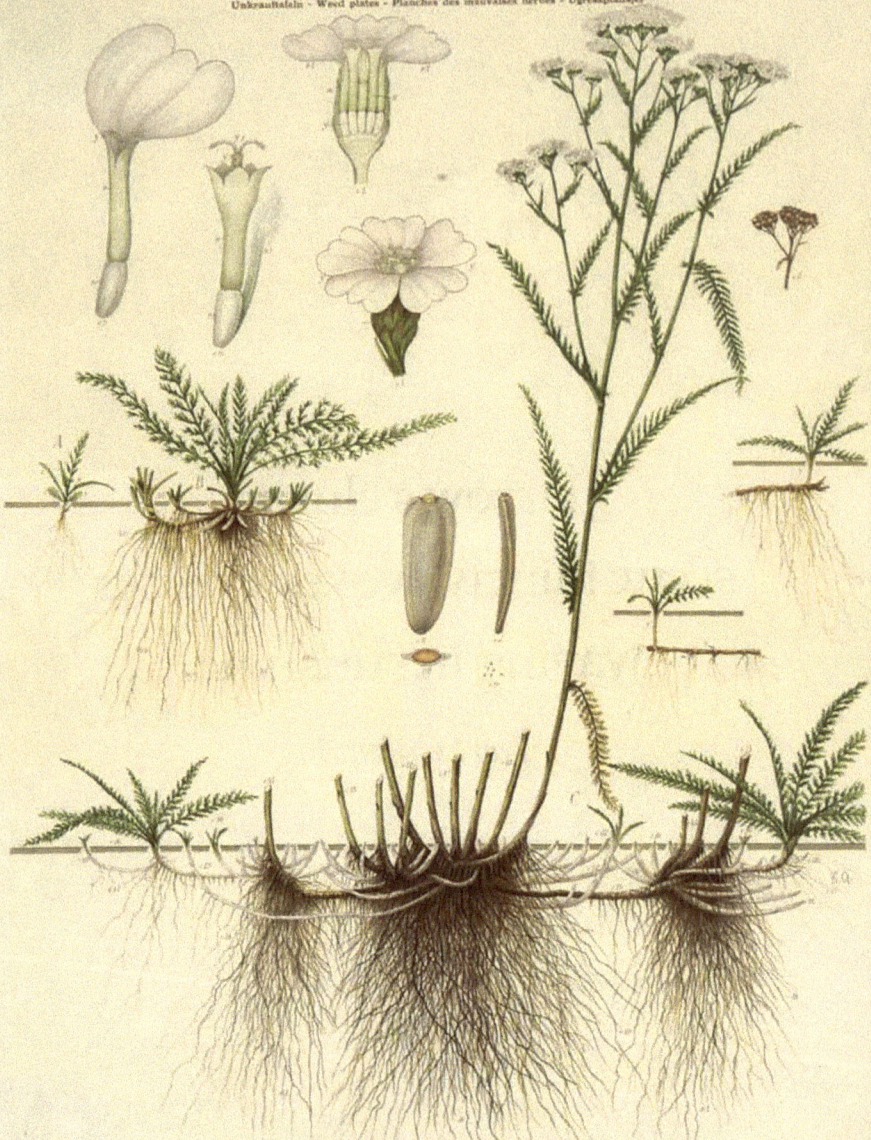

E. Korsmo. *Achillea millefolium* L. *Weed Plates.* 1934-1938.
Public Domain, plantillustrations.org

The Natural History of *Achilllea*

Kathleen Connole

Achillea is a member of the Asteraceae family, which contains over 1600 genera and some 23,600 species worldwide, and today is found on every continent on earth except Antarctica. The oldest pollen samples of Asteraceae to date have been found in Patagonia, dating back 65 to 50 million years ago, when this now subarctic region was home to tropical forests. Patagonia, New Zealand, Australia, and Antarctica, which are in the world's highest latitudes in the southern hemisphere, witnessed the early evolution of this plant family.

Asteraceae is the most diverse group within the angiosperms, the flowering plants. Characteristics such as a relatively short generation time, rapid population growth, and the close association with insect pollinators gave these plants an adaptive advantage over the more ancient gymnosperms. The family Asteraceae was and is of major influence in "the diversification and evolution of large numbers of animals that rely on their inflorescences to survive" (Barreda, www.doi.org). (Including humans.) The most recent common ancestors of this plant family were present in the supercontinent called Gondwana, 80 million years ago. During the late Paleocene and early Eocene, 60 to 50 million years ago, as the climate warmed, there was a dramatic rise in the diversity of flowering plants.

This history explains the fact that *Achillea* is considered circumboreal—native to northern temperate regions worldwide, on continents that are now separated by the earth's oceans. *Achillea millefolium* has the widest range of all the species and is one of the oldest herbs known to be used medicinally by humans, before written history.

There is archeological evidence of the importance of yarrow to very early humans as both medicinal and ceremonial plants. The Shanidar Cave burial site in Iraq that dates from 60,000 to 80,000 years ago was found to include the flower heads of eight species of medicinal plants, including yarrow. It is believed to be the grave of a traditional healer, as there were other burial remains without any plants. The other examples were found in Spain, in the

El Sidron Cave. Chemical analysis of dental calculus taken from 49,000-year-old remains revealed microscopic bits of plant material that contained azulenes and coumarins, substances found in yarrow and chamomile. There was also evidence of cooked plant foods high in starch; yet the presence of the herbs with no nutritional value gives credence to the theory that "the Neanderthal occupants of El Sidon had a sophisticated knowledge of their natural surroundings, which included the ability to select and use certain plants for their nutritional value and for self-medication" (Hardy, www.ncbi. nim.nlm.hih.gov).

There are multiple *Achillea millefolium* subspecies and varieties common to North America, from the Appalachians to California, and as far north as Alaska. Yarrow is one of the most common and widely known wildflowers, especially in the Great Plains of the western United States and Canada.

There are still sources that state that yarrow is not native to North America and was introduced as *A. millefolium* by European settlers. However, there are many indigenous language words for yarrow, none of which are borrowed from English, French, or Spanish languages. Yarrow has had a vital and long-standing role in traditional Native American herbalism; more so than such introduced herbs as dandelion and chicory (www.native-languages.org). It was known as "Warrior plant" by the Plains tribes, due to its well-known styptic properties. Yarrow was one of the Sacred Life Medicines of the Navajo nation and was burned as a purifying herb by the Anishinabe people. The Zuni used chewed yarrow juice from the blossoms and roots as a cooling wash after their fire juggling ceremony. The Hopi were the only group of the American southwest that are not documented to have used yarrow as medicine, but it could be that they just did not want to share such sacred knowledge with outsiders. In *The Cherokee Herbal, Native Plant Medicine from the Four Directions*, author J.T. Garrett lists yarrow in each of the sections on medicinal herbs of the East, South, West, and North. The uses listed are very much the same as those of cultures worldwide; one interesting use that is perhaps unique is "to stimulate the appetite of elders."

The species listed on the Native American Ethnobotany website include *Achillea millefolium arenicola*, *A. m.* var. *borealis*, *A. m.* var. *californica*, and *A. m.* var. *occidentalis* (formerly known as *A. lanulosa*). The tribes who are known to have used them, with over 377 distinct applications, are the Aleut, Anishinabe, Carrier, Cherokee, Cheyenne, Costanoan, Cree, Great Basin, Kawaiisu, Meskwaki, Montana, Milwaukee, Navajo, Ojibwa, Ottawa, Pauite, Pomo, Sanpoil, Saskatchewan, Shoshoni, Utah, Washo, Yurok, and Zuni. It is often listed as a "tonic" or "panacea" for almost any ailment.

Achillea lanulosa Nutt. (named by Thomas Nuttall, naturalist explorer of North America in the 1800s) was the species most widely used as medicine by the native peoples prior to European settlement. Although it is visually identical to *A. millifolium*, recent studies have revealed that *A. lanulosa* is genetically unique when compared to *A. millefolium* and its related species. The *A. millefolium* group is azulene-free, whereas *A. lanulosa* does contain azulene (Chandler 1982). This could explain why some have claimed that it is more medicinally potent for the treatment of certain specific conditions.

Yarrow is known to be an early successional plant, easily established and adaptable. It does not need to be pampered; in fact, the most potent essential oil compounds are produced when the plant is stressed.

Not only does yarrow possess multiple beneficial properties for the health of humans, but it also has some amazing qualities that can help our planet. Yarrow is called a "dynamic accumulator." It is a good companion plant that attracts beneficial insects, and its aromatic compounds distract and dissuade harmful pests and diseases. Yarrow has deep roots that help break up compacted, dense soils. Nutrients such as phosphorus, potassium, and copper are concentrated in the leaves and released back into the soil as they decompose, aiding in the rehabilitation of disturbed sites (www.permacultureplants.com).

The recorded historic uses of yarrow as medicine are vast, from ancients such as Pliny and Dioscorides to the pharmacopoeias of the 1800s. In the 1980s a Roman ship from 140 to 120 BCE, that sank off the coast of Tuscany, was found to contain medical supplies, including pressed tablets of plant material. DNA analysis revealed that these plants included yarrow, along with several others known to be used medicinally at that time. There are old English medical texts from 950 to 1000 CE, mostly translations of earlier Latin works, that recommend yarrow. There are many folk remedies using yarrow common to the countries of Northern Europe. It has been part of Traditional Chinese Medicine for centuries.

We are all familiar with the origin of yarrow's botanical genus name, *Achillea*. *Achilles heel* is a term that we have also heard many times. Some legends say that Achilles was dipped into a vat of yarrow tea; others say that it was the River Styx. Either way, he was held by his heel, which meant that he was thus vulnerable. The name *Achillea* was officially given to yarrow by Linnaeus in his work, *Species Plantarum*, in 1753.

Yarrow has become naturalized in many regions of the Southern Hemisphere. It is valued for its medicinal properties in Central and South America,

Majestic yarrow can grow up to heights of 5 or 6 feet. *Susan Belsinger*

the northern regions of the Amazon, South Africa, Botswana, and the Pacific islands. In Indonesia yarrow is used against malaria (Applequist and Moerman 2011). Since *Achilllea* readily hybridizes, there is much "taxonomic confusion" (Chandler et al., 1982) over the genetic differences in species growing wild today. This has caused dilemmas in interpreting the results of studies of the medicinal properties, as most refer to the common name yarrow, or *Achillea millefolium*, even though they might have been subspecies or hybrid varieties. It has been found that certain factors can affect and cause variations in the same species' growth habit and constituents, such as environmental conditions, altitude, the age of the plant, the part or parts used, and the season of collection.

Although there have been few scientific studies of the efficacy of yarrow in human clinical trials, the widespread evidence of medicinal uses by so many different cultures worldwide, from ancient times to the present, can be interpreted as validation.

In the words of Dr. James Duke, " ... plants used by unrelated groups for similar purposes are especially likely to be effective ... a plant whose use is independently adopted and retained by multiple cultures has an increased likelihood of being genuinely bioactive" (Applequist and Moerman 2011).

In the article titled "Yarrow: A Neglected Panacea? A Review of Ethnobotany, Bioactivity, and Biomedical Research," the authors conclude that "animal studies and extensive human experience indicate that, for those who are not allergic to it, yarrow is safe and well tolerated ... The time has come for this ancient medicine to take its place in the modern pharmacopeia, and science must rise to the challenge" (Applequist and Moerman 2011).

References

Applequist, W.L., Moerman, D.E. "Yarrow: A Neglected Panacea? A Review of Ethnobotany, Bioactivity, and Biomedical Research." *Economic Botany*, Vol. 65 No. 2, 15 June 2011. pp. 209-225. www.jstor.org/stable/41242932. Accessed 11-6-23.

Barreda et al. "Early Evolution of the Angiosperm clade Asteraceae in the Cretaceous of Antarctica." *Proceedings of the National Academy of Sciences of the USA*, 2015. www.doi.org/10173/pnas.1423653112. Accessed 10-28-23.

Boyle, A., Science Editor, *NBC News.* "Scientists find medicinal plants caught in Neanderthal teeth." 18 July 2012. www.nbcnews.com. Accessed 10-24-23.

Chandler et al. "Ethnobotany and Phytochemistry of Yarrow, *Achillea millefolium*, Compositaea." *Economic Botany*, Vol.36, No. 2 (Apr.-Jun. 1982) pp. 203-223. www.jstor.org/stable/4252376. Accessed 11-6-23.

Hardy, K. "Paleomedicine and the Evolutionary Context of Medicinal Plant Use." 9 Oct. 2020. www.ncbi.nim.nlm.nih.giv/pmc/articles/PMC7546d135/. Accessed 10-24-23.

Moerman, D. *Native American Ethnobotany*, NAEB Database, 2023. www. naeb.brit.org/uses/search/?string=Achillea. Accessed 11-3-23.

Sommer, J.D. (1999) "The Shanidar IV 'Flower Burial': A Re-evaluation of Neanderthal Burial Ritual." *Cambridge Archeological Journal 9*, pp. 127-129. www.journals.cambridge.org/abstract_SO959774300015249. Accessed 10-24-23.

Quanstrom, R. "Yarrow, *Achillea millefolium*." www.permacultureplants. com. Accessed 10-24-23.

Kathleen Connole joined the Ozark Folk Center's Heritage Herb Garden team in 2006. Before moving to Arkansas' Buffalo River Country in 2005, Kathleen earned a degree in Plant Science from the University of Missouri-Columbia and worked at Powell Gardens and Farrand Farms in Kansas City, Missouri. Kathleen researches the natural history of the Heritage Herb Garden's diverse herbal collection. She composes interpretive signage for the Garden to tell the stories of these plants. Kathleen served as chair and is an active member of the Herb Society of America Ozark Unit, headquartered at the Ozark Folk Center State Park. She currently is secretary for the International Herb Association Board. She was editor of the IHA's *Viola, Herb of the Year™ 2022, Ginger, Herb of the Year™ 2023, Yarrow, Herb of the Year™ 2024* and is currently working on *Chamomile, Herb of the Year™ 2025*.

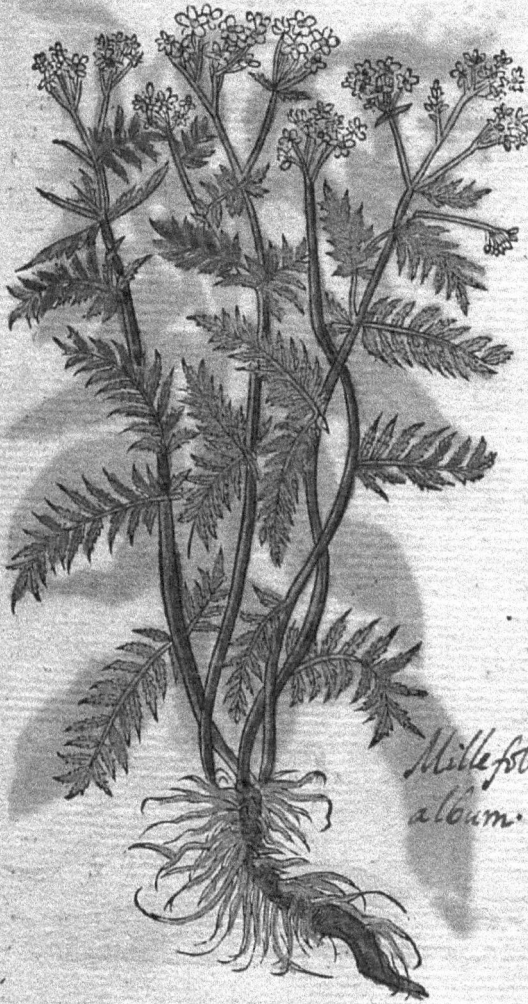

Αχίλλειος Latinis Achillion aut Achillea, nōnullis Achillea sideritis, alijs Diodela. Officinis persperam Milefolium: Germanis, Garb/ Schaff=garb/ Schaff=ryp/vnd Tausent=blatt. Brabantis, Geruwe Gallis Mil lefueille.

Millefolium vulgare album. Pin.

Woodblock print. *Achillea millefolium* L. Dodonaeus, R. *Stirpium historia commentariorum*, 1553-1554. *Public Domain, plantillustrations.org*

Field mice enjoy nibbling wild yarrow flowers. *Skye Suter*

Yarrow Yarb Tales from the Ozarks

Tina Marie Wilcox

I got intimately acquainted with *Achillea* in the late 80s as the new Heritage Herb Garden was planted at the Ozark Folk Center State Park in Mountain View, Arkansas. Yarrow lived up to its species name, *millefolium*, as the plants with multipennate leaves spread and established large patches in the first summer. Many visitors asked what kind of ferns they were. Maybe the short stature of the plants when not in bloom, paired with the soft, fernlike leaves, caused the confusion.

Rose (or pink) yarrow took to our habitat of poor sandstone atop the park's mountain. It adapted happily to partially shaded garden spots. It didn't mind having its bare rhizomes moved, in the height of summer, if the gardener kept the transplants moist for a couple of weeks until new roots could form. Pink yarrow filled many a vacant space left by more finicky, dead herbs. It is also pugilistic, holding its own even as horsetail (*Equisetum arvense*), blue violet (*Viola sororia*), and Bermuda grass (*Cynodon dactylon*) invade its territory. Neglected plantings of yarrow can be rescued and replanted when the ground is moist. An observant gardener will be able to identify the difference between the long, slender rhizomes of yarrow and the underground parts of the invaders as sections of the soil are lifted with a spade and then carefully broken apart.

Conversely, golden (or yellow) yarrow refused to take hold, no matter how many times or in how many different places it was planted. I really wanted it to like us because dried flowers, known as everlastings, were all the rage in those decades. The garden produced some revenue by selling dried flowers in bundles or using them to decorate swags and wreaths. Yellow yarrow retains its color and form better than the pink and white varieties. I was very jealous of my friend, Jackie Leatherman, who grew a grand stand of yellow yarrow on a spacious, sunny island near the parking lot of Cooper Park in Mountain Home, Arkansas, when she was a supervisor in the city's parks department. I think yellow yarrow needs lots of space and full sun to thrive.

I often came across white yarrow in Ozark pastures while botanizing with my herbal teachers. I thought of it as common, maybe too common, for our public garden. My views about wild plants and their place in our gardens have radically changed for the sake of native pollinators, beneficial predators and moths and butterflies.

Even though white yarrow has been planted in the garden several times in recent years, it has not established a forever home here—yet. After it was planted, the patch would last for maybe two or three years and then disappear. Perhaps, as is usual with the Herb of the Year™ program, deep research into a single genus will reveal this plant's growing requirements. Come to think of it, I find this plant growing in full sun, poor soil, receiving water only when it rains, and coexisting happily with a mixture of grasses and forbs. Maybe cultivated, enriched, and irrigated garden soil is just too rich for this tough *Achillea* species. I am setting intent in 2024, for this Herb of the Year, that white yarrow will set down roots in one of our native plant gardens and decide to stay.

It turns out that white yarrow belongs in one of our native plant gardens. Over the years there has been an ongoing disagreement between botanists, gardeners, and herbalists as to the origins of white yarrow. A plant that is commonly found in wild places is not necessarily native to the region. Some wildflower field guides and herbal references then and even now state that yarrow is native to Europe or Eurasia, while others claimed it was native to North America and other temperate regions. Finally, the Arkansas Native Plant Society, a group of botanists paired with native plant enthusiasts, settled the question in the ANPS Blog, "Know Your Natives" for yarrow on February 13, 2020. According to these learned people, white yarrow is " … native to North America, Asia and Europe—one of the largest worldwide ranges among flowering plants."

Regardless of the variety, when it comes to cultivating yarrow in a public garden, it is my stringent rule that the bloom stems must be cut flush with the crowns of the plants when harvesting the flowers or deadheading. It is poor form to leave stubs sticking up from the patch. This undisciplined whacking is unsightly, and the sharp nubs prick the hands of those who stroke the leaves to detect yarrow's fragrance. If you cut yourself with your pruners or on sharp bloom stems left by a careless gardener, just use yarrow leaves as a first aid bandage.

Long ago, early in the month of July, I was deadheading yarrow one fine evening, when Dave Smith hurried by on his way to the Ozark Highland

Wild yarrow in author's yard "battling it out with the Bermuda grass."
Tina Marie Wilcox

Theater to emcee the evening music show. I called out, "Hey Dave!" and couldn't help but notice conspicuous bits of white tissue paper stuck to his handsome face. Though Dave's voice and great talent dancing, storytelling and playing guitar and fiddle could have landed him a musical career in Nashville, he chose instead to build a cabin on his farm with his wife and keep their two boys close to nature. As usual, he was probably mending fences or building a zip line for his sons that afternoon and had to rush to be on time for the show. Before dressing in his starched white band collar shirt, suspenders, and vintage trousers, he quickly shaved his four o'clock shadow. Like many men, when he nicked his face, he just tore pieces of tissue paper and stuck them, with the help of sticky blood, on the cuts, to staunch the bleeding.

I pinched off foliage of yarrow, jumped up and ran to catch him, pressing the leaves into a moist, green mash with my thumb on the palm of my other hand. When we reached backstage, I caught my breath, gave him the poultice, and recommended he replace the tissue paper with small wads of yarrow. He thanked me profusely because although he didn't go in for herbal cures, he was still bleeding and had forgotten all about the close shave in his hurry. We couldn't have him on stage with toilet paper on his face! By the time he stood in the spotlight to welcome the audience, his face was free of poultices and there was not a trace of blood. You fellers remember that remedy the next time you need it.

We held three seasonal Heritage Herb Garden educational events in the 1990s. The park's 1994 Herb Harvest Fall Festival was a three-day symposium that featured Madalene Hill and Gwen Barclay, authors of *Southern Herb Gardening* and Deborah Duchon, founder of the journal, *The Wild Foods Forum*.

I savored my first taste of yarrow during Deborah Duchon's demonstration of Yarrow Tempura that weekend. I do not have her recipe. It was a simple process of dipping yarrow leaves in tempura batter and frizzling them in hot oil. The leaves were crunchy and tasted like yarrow smells, combined with the flavor of fried tempura batter. It was a fun and tasty novelty.

In searching for her recipe online I learned that she passed away in 2019. Ms. Duchon's life's work with plants and nutrition was extensive. I am grateful to her because she was a conduit for the preservation of ancient knowledge. *The Wild Foods Forum* was part of my herbal education, and she published one of my stories. Yarrow connected many students of herbs at our event with Deborah Duchon, in person. *Achillea* is a fine example of the Heritage Herb Garden's vision: "Where people and plants connect in the Ozarks."

References

Arkansas Native Plant Society. *"Know Your Natives - Yarrow."* https://anps.org/2020/02/13/know-your-natives-yarrow/#:~:text=Yarrow%20(Achillea%20millefolium)%20of%20the,ranges%20among%20the%20flowering%20plants. Accessed 9 August 2023.

Tina Marie Wilcox has been the head gardener and herbalist at the Ozark Folk Center State Park's Heritage Herb Garden in Mountain View, Arkansas since 1984. She co-authored the reference book *the creative herbal home* with Susan Belsinger.

Tina currently serves as president of The International Herb Association, a professional business organization that founded the Herb of the Year™ program. She is a Rosemary Circle member of the Herb Society of America and was honored in 2017 with the Society's Nancy Putnam Howard Award for Excellence in Horticulture.

Tina's herb and gardening philosophy is based upon experiencing the joy of the process, perpetrating no harm, and understanding life through play with plants and people.

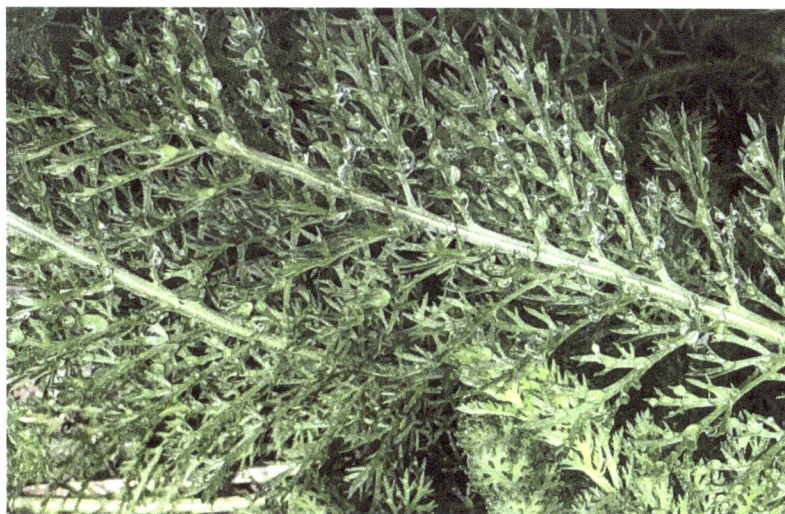

The use of yarrow leaves to stop bleeding is one of its most ancient uses.
Susan Belsinger

Close-up view of wild yarrow, Stone County, Arkansas. *Tina Marie Wilcox*

Germinating White-Flowering Yarrow Seeds

Tina Marie Wilcox

Many herb groups participate in the Herb of the Year™ program. The Herb Society of America-Ozark Unit is no exception. In anticipation of yarrow's designation as the 2024 Herb of the Year, member Lana Zirbel gave the Heritage Herb Garden a 1/4-ounce package of the seed of *Achillea millifolium,* common yarrow, which has white flowers, though some occasionally have a pink tinge.

Lana purchased the seeds from Sauder Farm Country Market. The germination rate on the package was listed as 90% and packed for 2023. This was a generous gift of a copious quantity of tiny yarrow seeds!

Because white-flowered yarrow is a native perennial, I immediately wondered if the seeds would need a period of moist stratification. My Google search resulted in numerous recommendations for a one-month cold stratification period. Some sources said that the seed needed a cold period before planting. Others stated that the seeds needed moist stratification, indicating the seeds need to be mixed with moist growing medium or sand and either planted outside or stored in the crisper of the refrigerator for 30 days.

I then opened *The Medicinal Herb Grower: A Guide for Cultivating Plants that Heal*, Volume 1, by Richo Cech. Richo really does grow herbs and has done so for many decades. This book was published in 2009. The book is all about seed germination, critical thinking, common sense, observation, experimentation, ingredients for custom growing medium blends; it does not have an index. I'd recommend it to all gardeners who want a quick and entertaining guide to understanding plants and what they need.

Inspired by Richo's book, I decided to perform an experiment. Lana's seeds had never, to my knowledge, seen the inside of a refrigerator. The package was stored at more or less 70°F between sometime in late summer until

November 15, 2023, the day of sowing the seeds. Two standard nursery flats were placed inside webbed flats. The flats were filled with sifted and moistened Promix BX, which is general purpose, soilless growing medium inoculated with biofungicide and mycorrhizae. Each flat was broadcast with 1/16th teaspoon of the yarrow seeds. Even this tiny measure resulted in a thickly seeded flat.

One flat was placed on a heat mat set to 70°F. A mist system emits three bursts of mist for five minutes, three times, between noon and 3:30 p.m. The flat was sprinkled with *Bacillus thuringiensis* var. *israelensis* (Bt) granules to protect emerging roots from damage by fungus gnat larvae.

The second flat was watered with a solution of Bt. We make Bt tea by filling 5-gallon buckets with water. The water stands for about 24 hours to allow the chlorine to evaporate, then 1/4-teaspoon of the granules are sprinkled in to grow the bacteria. This same product is used to treat standing water to kill mosquito larvae. The flat was then covered with a clear plastic dome and set on a shelf inside the park's unheated walk-in hoophouse.

Germination of the yarrow seeds on the heat mat was observed on November 19, 2023, just four days after sowing. The hoophouse flat germinated the very next day. Germination does appear to be at least 90% in both flats. True leaves were observed on the seedlings inside the greenhouse on December 1, 2023. The hoophouse yarrow matured to the true leaf stage several days later.

Thinning will be necessary to transplant the seedlings into 3-1/2 inch pots. We only need three flats of starter pots for sales and planting in the park.

The moral of this story is, one cannot believe everything that is repeated on the internet. The very best way to really know how to do most things is to first confer with trusted, known sources and then do your own experimentation.

Tina Marie Wilcox bio on page 27

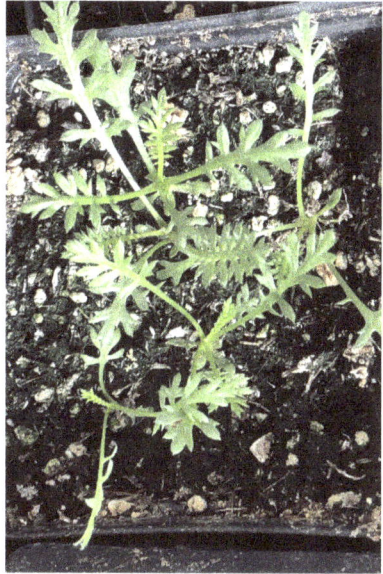

Young seedlings of yarrow. *Susan Belsinger*

Wild yarrow going to seed. *Gert Coleman*

Pollinators are drawn to the tiny flowers of yarrow. *Susan Belsinger*

Birds, Bees, and Butterflies
Love Yarrow

Diann Nance

Achillea species and the cultivated varieties of yarrow are the perfect plants if you want to attract pollinators to your garden. No matter what part of the country or the world you garden in, there is probably a variety of yarrow that is native there. The colorful flowers, known as corymbs (See Susan Belsinger's article, "Knowing Yarrow."), are attractive to many nectar-loving pollinators. Small birds, bees, and butterflies can easily sit on the flowers as they enjoy the nectar, pollen, and/or seeds from the blooms.

Hummingbirds might prefer longer-throated blooms, but when summer fries the southern US, more delicate plants give up their blooms to the heat while yarrow continues to spread its color and abundant nectar for hungry pollinators. Seed-loving small birds like finches can find yarrow seeds available throughout the growing season. Although you may want to deadhead throughout the growing season to encourage blooming, stop deadheading in late summer to leave seeds for the winter foraging birds.

The wild nature of yarrow makes it a desirable plant for bees. Yarrow will grow best on its own without interference from people. It is fun to imagine that bees love the hunt and discovery of a delicious source of nectar. They can even sit and rest for a while on the domed feast of tightly clustered flower heads. Honey bees enjoy yarrow and, like most of you, I love honey, and honey bees need to be protected; however, we need also to be concerned about our native bees. While honey bees get the majority of attention, bumble bees, orchard bees, carpenter bees, and many other bee pollinators are being overlooked and treated like they are menaces and expendable. Let's protect them too. If you don't like the kind of ragged nature of yarrow in your neatly pruned garden, find a wild spot where you can plant it and let it be found by native pollinators. Because they will find it. Other insects like flies and wasps will also feed on yarrow. Beneficial insects like ladybugs and lacewings may also be found around yarrow, although it is not thought to be a food source for them.

The colors, fragrance and shape of yarrow blooms make it especially beneficial to butterflies. According to Colorado State University, butterflies can see many more color shades than humans. This factor makes color extremely important when foraging for flowers to feed on. The colors they like best are bright, like orange, yellow, purple, red, and pink. Common wild yarrow is creamy white; however, there are cultivars in many bright shades. Some varieties which have contrasting central stamens are marketed as helping to attract butterflies to the heart of the flower. One such cultivar is 'Cerise Queen', a striking maroon beauty.

The shape of the flower with dozens of small blooms allows the butterfly to sit and sun itself for a long time feasting on the abundance of nectar. The spicy scent (similar to that of chrysanthemums) of yarrow may not be attractive to many humans, but it seems to be particularly attractive to butterflies. Night-time feeders such as moths will relish the creamy white yarrow.

Although yarrow is without a doubt an important food source of nectar for butterflies, I had to do more research to find out if yarrow is a host plant for any species of butterfly. Butterflies are very particular about where they lay their eggs. The plant has to be a source of green food for the developing larvae. Colorado State University lists a number of plants as hosts for the painted lady, which is why this butterfly is so numerous. Robert Frankson states that yarrow is the favorite host plant for the painted lady butterfly (*Vanessa cardui*), a member of the family Nymphalidae. The natural habitat of the painted lady includes flower meadows, countrysides, clover fields, sunny places, disturbed areas, roadsides, and dry open areas.

The painted lady butterfly can be found on every continent except Antarctica and Australia. In American butterfly books the painted lady butterfly is also referred to as American lady. Norman on his website "Understanding the painted lady butterfly," describes this garden beauty as "having pale orange to the upper wings, black tips are on the forewings marked with spots that are white. Rows of black spots can be found on the hindwings, and blue eyespots which are pale can be found on their undersides." Although the painted lady is a rather common butterfly here in Tennessee, I haven't found any larvae on the yarrow in my garden. But now that there are clumps of yarrow, I will keep a closer watch for painted lady caterpillars.

Grow a healthy yard with a variety of plants that attract and feed beneficial bees, birds, butterflies, and other insects. Sure, there will be some holes eaten in a few leaves. But maybe you will have fed painted lady larvae with that wild and lovely yarrow.

References

"Collecting and Sharing Data about Lepidoptera." 2023. www. butterfliesandmoths.org/. Accessed 1 August 2023.

Colorado State University. "Painted Lady." www.webdoc.agsci.colostate. edu/bspm/anthorpodsofcolorado/painted-lady.bdf. Accessed 1 July 2023.

Dunn, Jon L. and Alderer, Jonathan, eds. *Field Guide to the Birds of North America*, 5 ed. National Geographic, 2006.

Frankson, Robert. "Do Butterflies Like Yarrow?" 13 June 2023. www. wildyards.com/how-to-attract-butterflies/. Accessed 15 June 2023.

National Audubon Society. *Field Guide to North American Butterflies*. Alfred A. Knopf, 1997.

Norman. "Understanding the Painted Lady Butterfly Life Cycle." 17 May 2022. www.gardenofedengardencenter.com/painted-lady-butterfly-life-cycle/. Accessed 4 July 2023.

Yazza, Valeria. "Do Bees Like Yarrow?" 25 April 2023. www.shuncy.com/ article/do-bees-like-yarrow. Accessed 1 August 2023.

Diann Nance, born and raised on a farm in north central Texas, is presently living and growing herbs among the beautiful rolling hills of north central Tennessee. After a forty-year teaching career which included time spent in Texas, Taiwan, Germany, and finally Tennessee, she realized a long-held dream of starting a plant-growing business. She enjoyed eleven years of providing a wide variety of herbal plants for her community. Although Diann is now retired from the business of herbs, she still grows and uses herbs on a regular basis. Her interest in herbs and their uses in our daily lives can be attributed to her mother and grandmother who loved plants and shared their knowledge of herbs and plants in general.

Diann continues this tradition by growing plants, conducting workshops, and demonstrating the uses of herbs. She is a Master Gardener, a member of Beachaven Garden Club, the Herb Society of America, and the International Herb Association. She is a lifelong learner and may be contacted at dinance40@gmail.com.

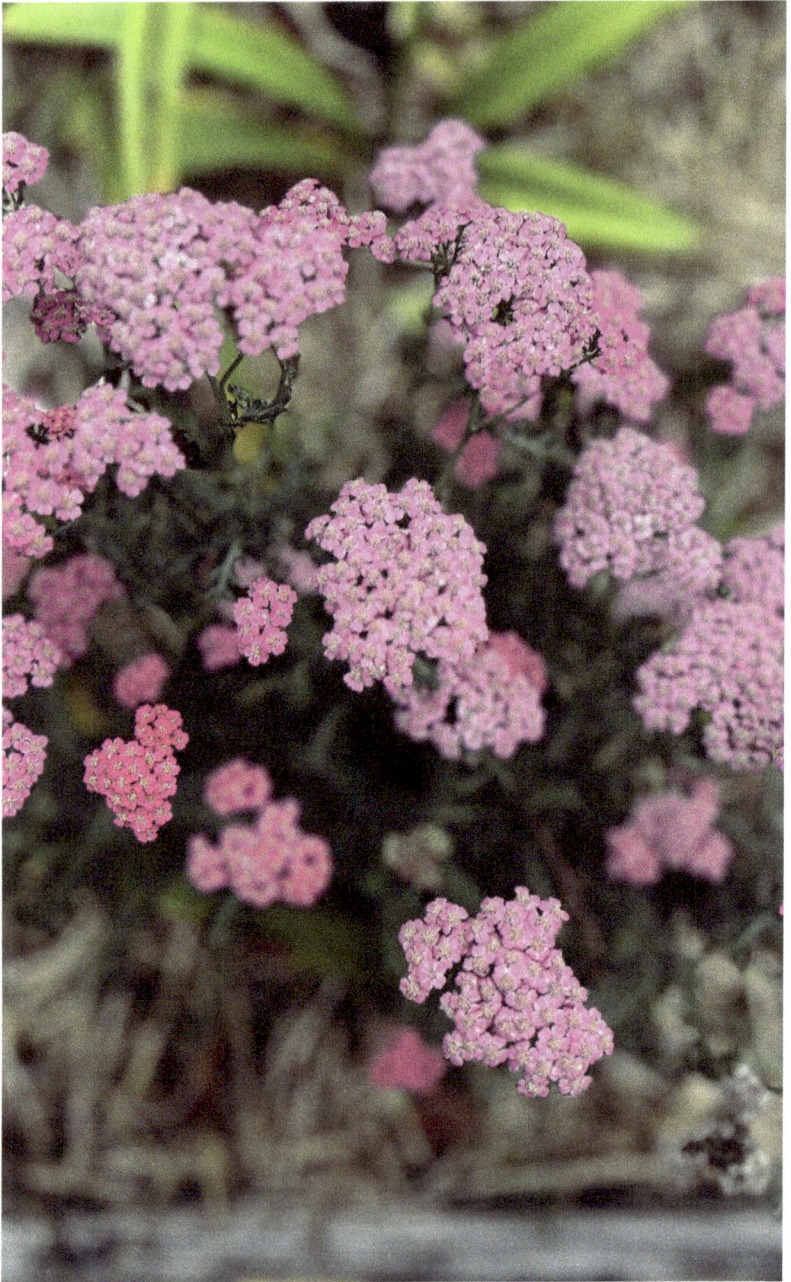

Yarrow cultivar in author's garden in North Florida. *Marge Powell*

Exploring the Yarrow Cultivars: Posing a Research Question

Marge Powell

Worldwide, there are more than 80 species of yarrow. Some have yellow flowers (*A. filipendulina, A. tomentosa, A. ageratum,* for example); some have more daisy-like flowers (*A. ptarmica, A. alpina, A. atrata*). Some grow in the mountains (*A. atrata, A. clavennae, A. erba-rotta*); some grow in sunnier climes (*A. arabica, A. abrotanoides, A. ligustica*); and some seem adaptable to many climates *(A. aegyptiaca, A. millefolium, A. nobilis*).

The *Achillea* genus is well populated, and we would expect many opportunities for hybridization. Hybridization involves the pollen of one species fertilizing the seeds of another species to produce hybrid seeds. This can often occur in nature and may result in a different variety of the species. Whereas a cultivar is a variation within a plant species that has been produced by human intervention to emphasize or de-emphasize certain plant traits. When looking at the name of the plant, if any part is not italicized, the assumption can be made that it is a cultivar. Cultivars are vegetatively reproduced; any seeds they produce will not replicate the parent plant. A cultivar can begin as a hybrid before the human intervention on the road to becoming a cultivar. Many yarrow cultivars started as a hybrid between *Achillea millefolium* and *A filipendulina.* In this discussion I refer to *Achillea millefolium* as common yarrow and collectively refer to the engineered plants as "cultivars" because to my knowledge I have not encountered any hybrids in this journey.

I have always had a healthy stand of yarrow, *Achillea millefolium*, in my garden. I have used it as an insect repellent in its tinctured form and straight out of the garden as a styptic. Years ago, I was having a party when a friend's date, whom I did not know, sliced open his finger on the pull tab of a beer can.

I quickly slipped out to my garden, pulled off a handful of yarrow leaves and hurried back to the house. The injured date was standing close to the back door in somewhat of a state of shock (after all he only wanted a beer and what he got was a profuse flow of blood down his hand). I grabbed his hand and wrapped the injured finger in the yarrow leaves. It's too bad no one took a picture of the look on his face when I did this. I quietly explained this would stop the bleeding and then we could get him cleaned up. The bleeding stopped, we cleaned him up, he regained his composure and said "I can't believe that worked. At first, I thought maybe you were a witch or something." Oh well, it was ever thus.

During my apprentice course with Susun Weed, she advised that for cleaning, we should brew an infusion of yarrow and spray it on surfaces to kill germs or alternately dilute a tincture for the spray. So, yarrow has always been on my herbal radar. But I confess to being a snob concerning the yarrow cultivars. My thought process went something like this. "An herbalist really wouldn't be concerned about those pretty things; they aren't even medicinal." I started to have a more open mind about a year ago when my husband brought back a plant he found at our local garden center. He said, "This was so pretty, it made me think you would like it." It was a yarrow cultivar and of course I planted it in my perennial garden and began to watch it develop and grow.

At first, my snobbishness took over and I barely tolerated the plant. But as its flowers and foliage matured, I began to use it as a cut flower. The pink cultivar flowers in a vase with the white flower heads of the common yarrow were quite beautiful.

This attitude melted away and I noticed these flowers more and more, especially as we traveled. We took a trip to Quebec, Canada, traveling from the Eastern Townships, then north along the St. Lawrence River to the Gaspe Peninsula and, of course, we visited gardens and there were many yarrow cultivars. In Sherbrooke, Quebec, which is plant hardiness Zone 5a, we saw this lovely patch of yarrow in front of the Fine Arts Museum.

Then we visited the Domaine Joly-De Lotbiniere garden, near Lotbiniere south of Quebec City. This is plant hardiness Zone 4a and the yarrows were stunning.

Then we traveled to one of the northernmost gardens in North America, Reford Gardens in Grand Metis, Quebec, which, according to their signage, is plant hardiness Zone 3. Again, the yarrow cultivars were standouts.

I garden in Zone 8b on the cusp of 9a in Northeast Florida. What amazed me is that I have seen healthy, thriving yarrow cultivars from Zone 3 all the

Yarrow cultivar, Zone 5A, Sherbrooke, QC. *Marge Powell*

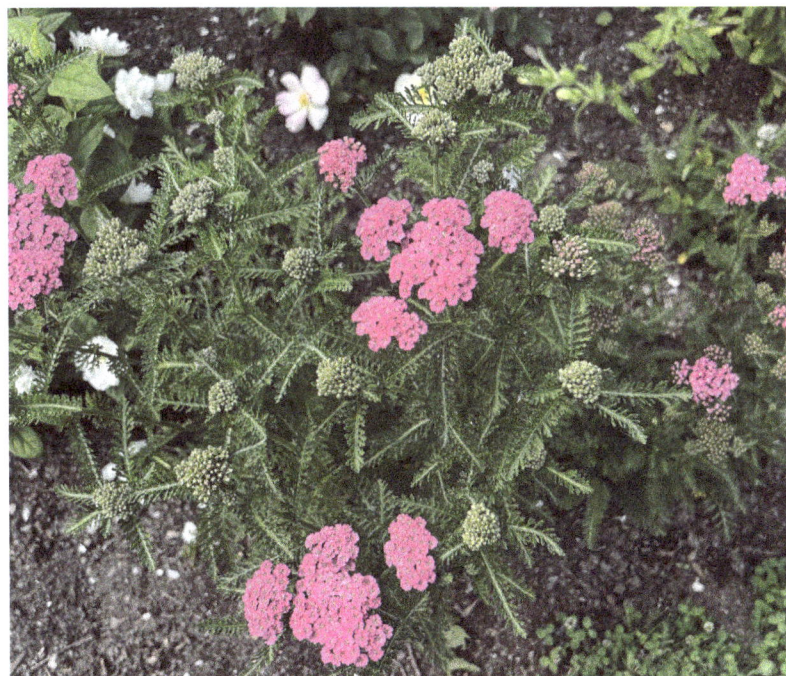

Yarrow cultivars, Zone 4A, Lotbiniere Garden, QC. *Marge Powell*

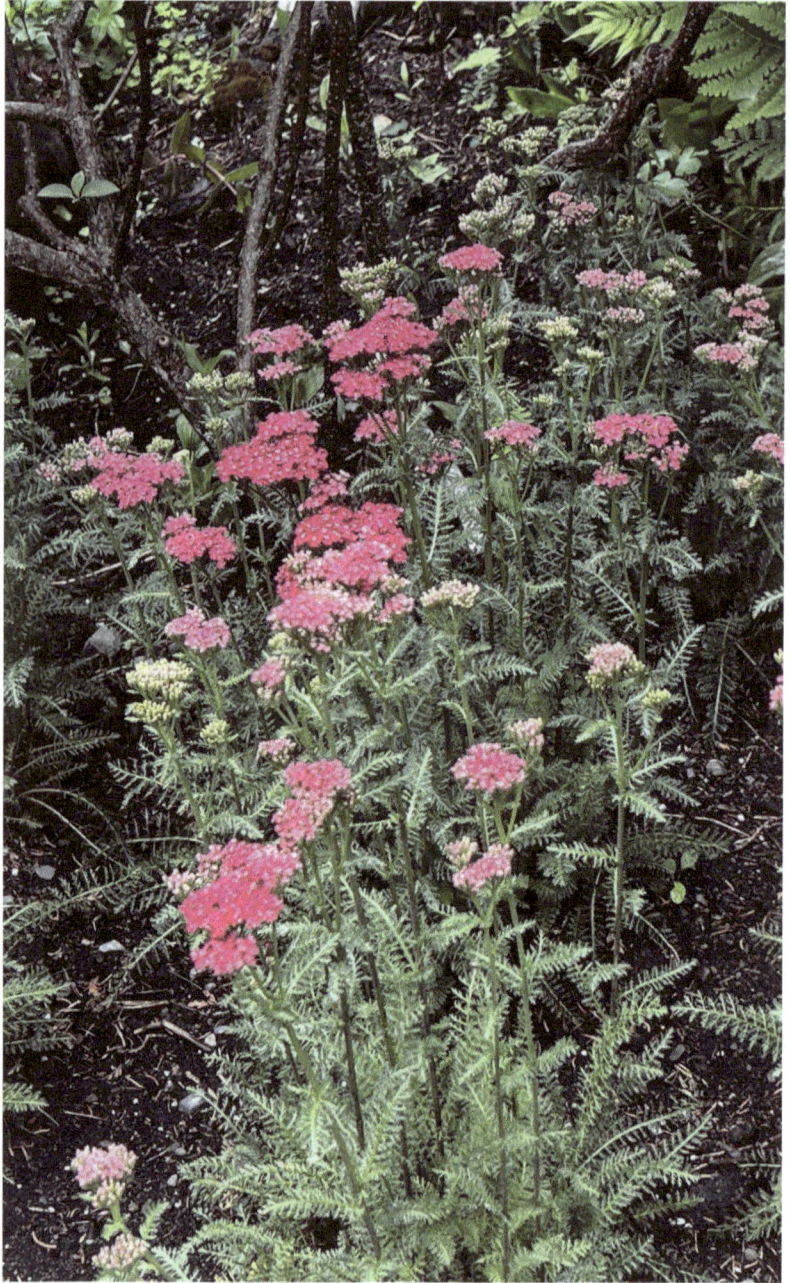

Yarrow cultivars, Zone 3, Reford Gardens, QC. M*arge Powell*

way to Zone 8b. I suspect only a minority of plants can claim that impressive range.

When we returned from this trip, I decided my garden would benefit from a few more of these yarrow cultivars which are rarely available in our local garden centers. I think it was a beneficial fluke that my husband found the one he did. So, I turned to the internet. The yarrow cultivar sources I found did not want to ship the plants to me because they said they would not grow in my agricultural zone. I had to agree to waive any guarantees and assume all the risk. They did ship, the plants have grown, and now I have a lovely patch of yarrow cultivars in a corner of my perennial garden. I bought two Proven Winners™, 'Firefly Peach Sky' and 'Firefly Diamond'. I also bought 'Red Velvet', 'Sassy Summer Sangria', 'Violet', and 'Firefly Sunshine'. The original plant from our local garden center was untagged. I also bought a Greek Yarrow, *Achillea ageratifolia,* a low growing white flowering plant described as "An excellent small-scale groundcover for planting in hot, sunny conditions." However, after two weeks in the garden it was apparent this plant was suffering. I potted it and placed it in my nursery in indirect light and it is doing well. I will plant it back in the garden in the fall when it is cooler.

The summer heat here in July and August dares anything to grow and thrive. I have consistently removed spent growth from my yarrow cultivars. The foliage is green and healthy but most of the blooming has ceased in the heat. There are emerging flower buds so I assume as the weather cools in the next few weeks blooming will resume. And one plant, 'Firefly Sunshine', continues to bloom even in this heat. Not a spectacular display, but healthy.

'Firefly Sunshine' in author's garden in August, North Florida. *Marge Powell*

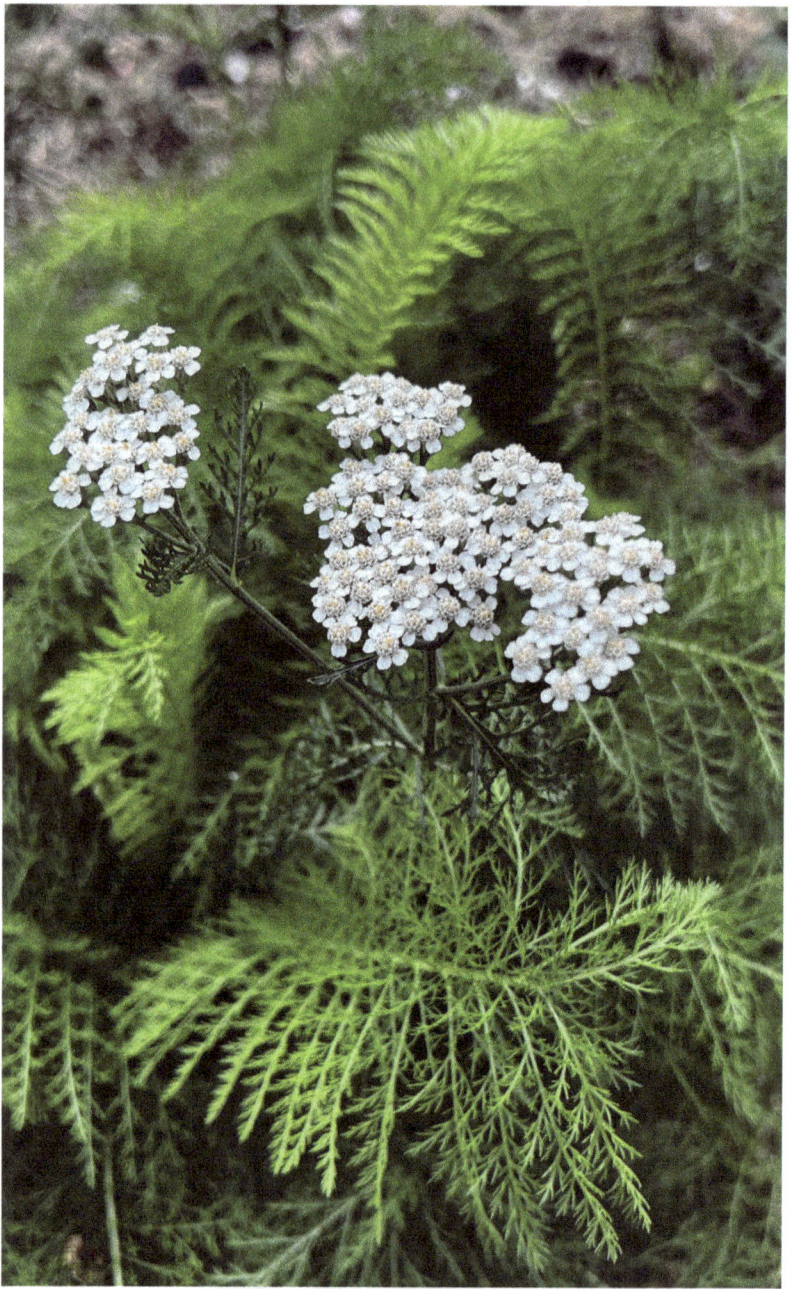

The leaves of common yarrow in the author's garden, North Florida.
Marge Powell

Posing a Research Question

I had been told through the years that the medicinal benefits were to be found only in the common yarrow, *Achillea millefolium*. But now I am asking myself: "Is this true?" Could it be possible that the cultivars also yield medicinal benefits?

I have made and sold herbal ointments, salves, and lotions for more than 24 years. Herbal ointments that I make are central to my self-care along with tinctures and infusions. But I never felt the need for a yarrow ointment until motivated by the question of possible medicinal benefits from the cultivars and because of what I learned in the process of researching applications for yarrow ointment.

In the literature yarrow is foremost promoted for its wound healing and usefulness with colds and fevers and stings and bites. David Hoffman states that yarrow can support the kidneys by increasing cleansing through the skin. But it is also used for cardiovascular support. It is said that the astringency of yarrow exerts a tonic influence on blood vessels and circulation which makes it helpful for shrinking hemorrhoids when used in a sitz bath. It was this latter application that interested me. I have no experience with hemorrhoids, but I do have experience with rosacea which has left spots of red veins on my face (which annoy me mightily).

My intent was to explore the topical effects rather than the internal effects of yarrow. I decided my approach would be an experiment using two ointments, as identical as possible: One made with leaves of common yarrow, and one made with leaves of yarrow cultivars. The literature also recommends using the blossoms of the yarrow plant, but the blossoms of my common yarrow were long gone, and it would skew the experiment if I used the cultivar blossoms. So, only leaves for the ointment, no blossoms. I hoped for two benefits from this experiment: first, understanding what benefits yarrow ointment in general might provide, and secondly, to see if there were any beneficial differences between the two ointments. I am not equipped with laboratory analysis apparatus so any conclusion I reach will be anecdotal, but I hope it will provide some insight into the medicinal properties of the common yarrow versus the yarrow cultivars.

In addition to the flower color, a distinguishing difference between the cultivars and the common yarrow is the leaves. The leaves of the common yarrow are larger and more feathery than those of the yarrow cultivars.

I decided the ointments would be small batches around two ounces each. The challenge in making the ointments would be to keep each ointment-making process identical.

1. I gathered the leaves and weighed them. Each batch weighed .35 ounces.
2. I dried the leaves in separate trays of my dehydrator at 95°F for exactly 10 hours. The outcome was that each batch of dried leaves weighed .10 ounces.
3. I infused each batch of leaves in 3 ounces organic extra-virgin olive oil.
4. The leaves infused at room temperature for exactly 5 weeks.
5. After 5 weeks, I decanted the infusions with these outcomes:
   · Common yarrow – 2.2 ounces of infused oil
   · Yarrow cultivar – 2.4 ounces of infused oil
   · I can't explain the difference in weight outcomes except perhaps the leaves of the common yarrow may have absorbed some of the oil.
6. I thickened the oils with natural beeswax to produce the finished ointments.* Normally I would have added essential oils to the ointments, but I did not want to cloud the experiment with an additional variable.
7. There was no color difference between the two ointments.

*I try to be thoughtful on the quantity of beeswax used to thicken ointments, and I have found it is not a linear relationship. My experience in making ointments has yielded the following graph:

Color consistency: Cultivar ointment on left, common yarrow ointment on right. *Marge Powell*

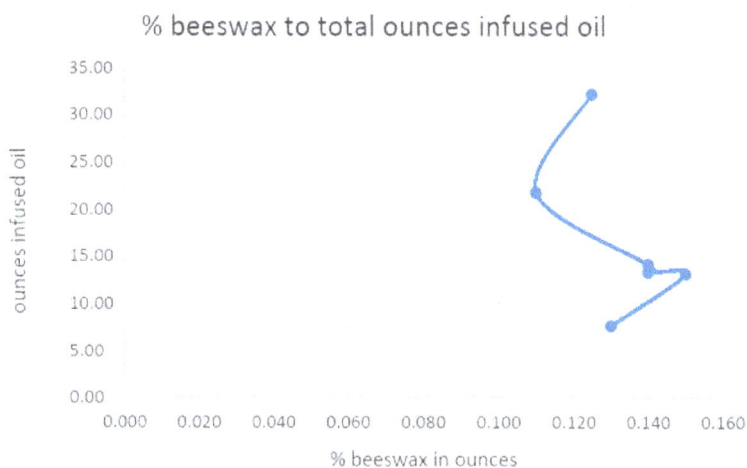

% beeswax to total ounces infused oil

ounces infused oil (y-axis: 0.00, 5.00, 10.00, 15.00, 20.00, 25.00, 30.00, 35.00)

% beeswax in ounces (x-axis: 0.000, 0.020, 0.040, 0.060, 0.080, 0.100, 0.120, 0.140, 0.160)

The smaller the ointment batch, the higher the percentage of beeswax is needed based on the weight of the oils. For these tiny batches I used 14% of the weight of the oil which meant the common yarrow batch was thickened with .3 ounces of beeswax and the cultivar batch with .34 ounces.

I applied the common yarrow ointment to the right side of my face and the cultivar ointment to the left side over a four-week period with the following results:

I was primarily interested in reducing the patch of red veins on my cheeks. My method was each morning I placed a fingertip of the common yarrow ointment on the right side of my face and a fingertip of the cultivar ointment on my left cheek. I was careful not to use the same finger when applying the ointment. After 6 weeks I am more than pleased with the results. The red veins are gone from each cheek. It seems the cultivar ointment was slower in achieving the results, but in the end the results are the same. An argument could be posed that I am seeing the effects of the oil rather than the effects of the herb. But prior to this experiment I was using another ointment I made using the same oil and I did not see these results.

I also used the cultivar ointment on chafed skin and found it to be effective. But again, the argument could be made that it was the oil and not the herb. I did not have the opportunity to use the ointment on wounds (which is a good thing) or on bleeding but will do so in the future when it is appropriate.

My conclusion, which is anecdotal, is that an ointment made from yarrow leaves, both common and cultivar, can have a tonic influence on blood vessels and circulation, as described by David Hoffman, but the application can be expanded beyond hemorrhoids. I also conclude that the cultivar ointment, while effective, requires a longer period of use than the common yarrow ointment to achieve similar results.

What I may do in the future is compose an ointment of common yarrow leaves with the addition of both cultivar and common yarrow flowers.

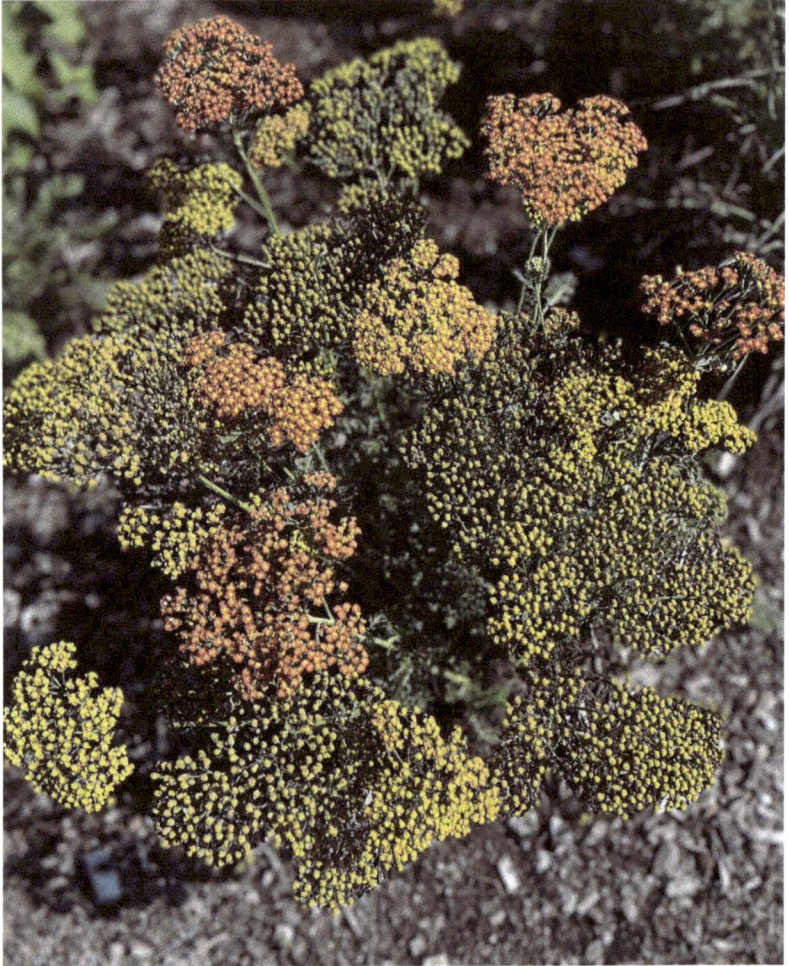

Yarrow cultivar in Maine Coast Botanical Garden, Boothbay, Maine.
Marge Powell

References

Bennett, Robin Rose. *The Gift of Healing Herbs*. North Atlantic books, 2014.

Hoffman, David. *The Herbal Handbook*. Healing Arts Press, 1988.

Love and Homemaking. "Yarrow Salve Recipe & Uses (Herbal Wound Healing Salve)." www.loveandhomemaking.com/yarrow-salve-recipe-uses/. Accessed 17 August 2023.

The Outdoor Apothecary. Barbi Gardiner. "Crafting Yarrow Salve: Honoring the Medicinal Gift of Achillea millefolium." www.outdoorapothecary.com/yarrow-salve/. Accessed 17 August 2023.

Verywell Health. Megan Nunn, PharmD. "What Is Yarrow? An Herb Studied for Wound Care, Inflammation, and Menstrual Pain." www.verywellhealth.com/yarrow-health-benefits-4586386#toc-uses-of-yarrow. Accessed 17 August 2023.

Marge Powell has been an herbalist for over 40 years and an avid plant person her entire life. Her herbal interests span both the culinary, the medicinal and body care as well as growing herbs. She completed a medicinal herbal apprenticeship with Susun Weed and was introduced to herbal body care in workshops conducted by Rosemary Gladstar.

Marge is a passionate cook and most of her cooking is herb-enhanced. She teaches classes in cooking with herbs, making your own medicines, creating lotions and ointments, making soap, and blending scents. She has conducted hands-on workshops on these and a variety of other herbal topics across the United States. From 2000 until 2022 she owned and operated Magnolia Hill Soap Co., Inc., a producer of herbal soaps and ointments. In 2011 she created Magnolia Hill Nursery which wholesales organic herbs and heirloom vegetables to local garden centers.

She is currently a board member of the International Herb Association (IHA) and the International Herb Association Foundation and is past president of IHA's former Southeastern Region. She has authored numerous herbal articles published in IHA's annual *Herb of the Year* publications. Recently she has begun collecting data on the history of folk medicine in NE Florida and SE Georgia, hoping to shed some light on this often neglected and unstudied aspect of herbal lore.

Most common yarrow has white blooms, though often they are tinged pink; there are many shades of pink amongst the cultivars. *Susan Belsinger*

Poetry and Perimeters:
Yarrow for Setting Boundaries

Gert Coleman

Plants are storytellers that draw us into the natural world,
and some of these botanical revelations can be formative.
~ John Forti, *The Heirloom Gardener*

Plants have long been used as symbols or ways to interpret the natural world and our responses to it. Mystical, magical, and medicinal yarrow (*Achillea millefolium*) is a plant with powerful stories to tell. Also known as allheal, arrow root, bad man's plaything, bloodwort, carpenter's weed, death flower, devil's nettle, devil's plaything, dog daisy, hundred-leaved grass, knight's milfoil, military herb, nosebleed, old man's pepper, sanguinary, seven year's love, snake's grass, staunchweed, thousand seal, woundwort, and yarroway, yarrow is a revered herb wherever it is found, including in poetry.

As philosopher Ralph Waldo Emerson (1803-1882) once said, "The eye reads omens where it goes." From gardens to battlefields to poetry and lore, yarrow offers mythological, folkloric, poetic, protective, healing, and historical portents throughout many cultures.

A beautiful white flower with a stiff stem, yarrow has been associated with blood, wounds, and battlefields as well as the grief that comes with death and loss. Dried yarrow leaf, or *herba militaris*, was an integral part of soldiers' first aid kits as recently as the American Civil War and World War I. In the *Language of Flowers*, yarrow symbolizes war, conflict, and struggle.

A plant of Venus, yarrow has also been associated with creativity, love, and beauty. Yarrow juice was once rubbed into hair to make it curly and attract a mate, and the leaves and flowers were used to predict true love or prophesize marital fidelity. Yarrow and calendula flowers were sometimes woven into garlands placed above marriage beds or carried with rosemary in bridal bouquets to bring about seven years of true love, seven being a metaphor for a long time.

This lovely perennial has the notable distinction of being a protection against evil, sorcery, and, in contemporary herbalism, the tractor pull of another's emotions, pain, and misfortune. As such, yarrow has been used in divination rituals as both a grounding and protective force as well as to open the third eye and mind. Medieval folks used it to ward off harmful spells, wearing it in amulets or stringing it across doorways, above barn doors, and over baby cribs. It is hard to separate magic from medicine and religion since most healing practices began as divination, a plea to the gods for a sign or help or answers to difficult questions, with supporting intonations and rituals.

Yarrow in Poetry: Rhymes

Humans often look to nature and literature for signs or signals, and herbs and flowers can help to tell stories, act as symbols, and reinforce nature in literary settings. Like so many herbs prominent in legends and folklore, yarrow offers interesting layers of symbolism. While rarely a main character in poetry (except for Wordsworth's Yarrow poems, 1803 to 1831, where it's a river not a plant), yarrow functions as an able, supportive image, particularly with the struggle between life and death, healing and surviving, adapting and divining.

As a word, *yarrow* proves its poetic worth with resonance, rhyming with *arrow* (a narrow missile shot with a bow); *barrow* (a mound of rock and soil over remains of the dead); *harrow* (torment, hex, bedevil; a scary-looking cultivating tool with spikes to break up and smooth soil); *marrow* (the life force of bones or the innermost, essential core); *narrow* (contract or limit; a sense of the openings between skin and the world, our psyche and the mundane world); *sparrow* (an ubiquitous gray-brown songbird that portends death in Celtic lore); and *tarot* (a form of divination). What an introduction to this complex herb, weed, and wildflower.

Words conjure up images and deepen meaning, particularly words in rhymes, which aid memory. Before village healers had formal education or certifications, healing lore was handed down orally, typically in easy-to-remember rhymes recited secretly. Thus healing herbs like yarrow, familiar to rural populations, starred in rhymes, adages, and admonitions, which were repeated three, five, or seven times.

Where the yarrow grows,
There is one who knows.

Find the yarrow and the healer or healing would be there. Or how about, to attract love or rebuild a relationship, reciting this rhyme while cutting yarrow:

I cut thee, Yarrow,
So that love may grow.

For personal safety, yarrow can also act as an alarm system; if yarrow fluttered unexpectedly in your field or garden, it portended a sorcerer nearby. Simply holding yarrow in the hand was believed to allay fears. Carried in good luck charms, yarrow offered protection from evil:

Yarrow, Yarrow, tremble and sway
Tiny flowers bright and gay
Protect my garden night and day.

In Ancient Chinese folklore, yarrow was considered so powerful that "wolves, tigers, and poisonous plants would never be found near it" (Silverman168).

Fading memories and wildflowers

Besides its effective use in rhymes, yarrow's visual image contributes to natural settings in literature. This creamy white, occasionally pink, wildflower with an erect stem grows easily in meadows, fields, and byways. Waving in the grasses, alive with pollinators, yarrow conjures up sunny summer days. As the flowers fade to ghostly off-white, even grey-brown, they affirm seasonality, the coming of autumn's chill, heralding the harvest and the year's end, darkness, and even death.

The American poet Edward Arlington Robinson (1869-1935) used yarrow's transforming flowers to eulogize a beloved sea captain who went down with his crew a decade earlier in the elegy "Pasa Thalassa Thalassa." The poem's stark opening line, "The sea is everywhere the sea" accentuates their overwhelming struggle as they drown.

In the fourth stanza, Robinson juxtaposes the word *dusk* (twilight or end of daylight) with the fading flowers and grasses of late summer to lament the fading of his friend's presence in everyday life:

Roses have had their day, and the dusk is on yarrow and wormwood—
Dusk that is over the grass, drenched with memorial dew;
Trellises lie like bones in a ruin that once was a garden,
Swallows have lingered and ceased, shadows and echoes are all.

The beauty and freshness of roses are finished, just a memory now, while bitter herbs like yarrow and (especially) wormwood linger on stalks in the fading light of autumn. Robinson uses this plant imagery to depict his loss in a pastoral setting, away from the sea that took his friend, whose memory will soon fade: roses whose thorns prick with sadness, yarrow as symbol of wounds and the battle he lost to the sea, and wormwood the bitterest of bitter herbs. The narrator hopes the herbs will help him accept the loss of his friend and the "hard red face that only laughter could wrinkle."

Boundaries and regrouping

Yarrow's healing qualities span every continent and culture. So it is no surprise to see yarrow used for easing grief in "Hiawatha's Lamentation" (1855), part of a longer epic poem celebrating Native American traditions by Henry Wadsworth Longfellow (1807-1882).

Native Americans burned yarrow to cleanse a person's energy and protect against one's essence being leached out by negative influences. The Chippewas called yarrow's finely cut, bipinnate leaves *adjidamowano,* or *squirrel tail*, suggesting its long, narrow arc and ability to wave gracefully in the slightest breezes. In the American Southwest, it is known as *plumajillo,*

Hiawatha's Departure. Currier & Ives lithograph, U.S. Library of Congress. *Public Domain*

or *little feather* (Sanders 135). Feathers are protective and keep the warmth in and the weather out. One can easily imagine yarrow's feathery leaves helping to wave away negativity and troubles.

When his best friend Chibiabos drowns "in the deep abysses/of the lake of Gitche Gumee," Hiawatha suffers a terrible loss:

From the headlands Hiawatha
Sent forth such a wail of anguish,
Such a fearful lamentation,
That the bison paused to listen,
And wolves howled from the prairies ...

A "strong, wise, young man of great reputation" and the heart and soul of his community, Hiawatha spends seven weeks grieving, painting his face black, refusing food and drink. Sickened with sorrow and sequestered from the tribe, Hiawatha is in danger of losing his life essence. His community watches with concern, then comes together to help him, with rituals, talismans and pouches of healing:

Filled with magic roots and simples,
Filled with very potent medicines.

Hiawatha follows them to the Sacred Wigwam, silent but no longer lamenting:

There a magic drink they gave him,
Made of Nahma-wusk, the spearmint,
And Wabeno-wusk, the yarrow,
Roots of power, and herbs of healing ...

Beating drums, the elders and shaman chant and pray over Hiawatha until he is cured and able to reconnect with his community.

Longfellow emphasizes the healing power of aromatic plants and rituals in this passage with two plants well known to his 19th century readership, yarrow and spearmint, sold by the Shakers and long used in teas, tinctures, and healing formulas. Spearmint's sweet, pleasant taste combines well with yarrow's fresh, astringent tones to create a soothing tea. Hiawatha, parched, tired, and lachrymose, would have been able to drink this infusion without grimacing. Spearmint (*Mentha spicata*) would rehydrate his dry mouth, and its minerals and antioxidants would help his constitution to revive and relax, and thus regain cognition.

Achillea millefolium. Gail Wood Miller

Yarrow and spearmint can stimulate appetite, allowing Hiawatha to regain his strength. Meanwhile, yarrow would jumpstart his circulatory system, helping him to regain a sense of self and begin to heal. Yarrow can also ease "heartburn," both the physical and emotional suffering Hiawatha has undergone through grief.

While yarrow has traditionally been prescribed to stem bleeding, it can also staunch "metaphorical" bleeding. Herbalist Anne McIntyre calls yarrow "the flower of invulnerability" and recommends its flower essence for "those who are easily affected and depleted by their surroundings and the influence of others, and tend to be prone to environmental illnesses, allergies, and psychosomatic problems. It helps to shield from outside influences and reduce leakage of energy and absorption of negative influences" (259).

Perhaps, in Longfellow's poem, the elders should also drink Hiawatha's yarrow tea. Healers and healthcare workers, counselors and teachers—really, anyone who is empathetic to the struggles of others—might find yarrow an ally in their work, shielding them both physically and emotionally from the outpourings of their clients. Much of what we today call *burnout* might be alleviated by adding yarrow to our arsenal of protection. In *The Illustrated Herbiary*, Maia Toll asserts that yarrow "creates pockets of protection so you can slow down, gather your strength, and find your courage" to move forward (109). Perhaps that yarrow-spearmint infusion did just that for Hiawatha, helping him to recover from the ravages of grief and loss.

Herbalist Katje Swift agrees that yarrow can help healers to avoid the tug of another's pain: "Physiologically, we work with Yarrow for bleeding, and emotionally that can be true too—to prevent your own resources from bleeding out of you while you're supporting others. But the mythology behind Yarrow ... also plays a part: Yarrow is like 'emotional armor'. When you need to be strong in difficult situations, when you need to put on your armor and head out to the emotional battlefield, Yarrow has an amazing shielding quality."

Yarrow subtly reminds us to be aware of our own weaknesses and protect ourselves fully. Thus, yarrow helps us to question, create, and recognize boundaries in the community and relationships.

"Does yarrow call the fairies? Or do the fairies call forth yarrow?"
Susan Belsinger

The Mystical Garden: Fairies too

Yarrow's other mythical powers concern divination, clairvoyance, and exorcism. Sipping yarrow tea, perhaps mixed with basil, mint, thyme, or mugwort, can help us slip into meditative states or journey to hidden aspects of the psyche (*Magical Herbalism* 63). In the Hebrides, it was believed that holding a yarrow leaf against the eyes encouraged the "second sight" to emerge. Yarrow stalks have also been used to "reawaken the spiritual forces of the superconscious mind during ritual divination using the *I Ching*" (McIntyre 49).

In China, *A. millefolium's* cousin, *A. sibirica,* the famous *I Ching* "stalks of divination" were cut, dried, and sold in parcels of fifty, their length indicating the status of the users: stalks for the emperor were nine feet long; princes, seven feet; dignitaries and government officials, five feet long, and so on (Silverman 167). According to Gerina Dunwich in *Magick Potions*, yarrow has often been an integral part of rituals regarding ancestors, art, beauty, childbirth, family and home, friendships, healings, love, medicine, meditation, psychic power, and all forms of spirituality (150).

While medieval midwives used yarrow for its medicinal properties, they also employed its psychological or talismanic properties. According to Maida Silverman in *The City Herbal*, "To ease childbirth, Yarrow that had been gathered on St. John's or Midsummer Eve (June 21, the summer solstice, a day of great and powerful magical significance since ancient antiquity) was given to a woman in labor. She held it pressed to her right side, but it had to be taken away as soon as the child was born" (166). Having endured two difficult labors, I would have held tightly to yarrow if it had been given to me.

Herbalist Matthew Wood suggests a proactive, contemporary use of yarrow's magical healing that harks back to one of yarrow's names, *carpenter's weed.* Those who work with sharp tools like carpenters and metalsmiths "would do well to put a sprig of yarrow in the toolbox, or among the power tools. This sends a message that accidents are not welcome. One sprig in the spring and one in the fall is a good measure" (*Herbal Wisdom* 82). On a practical level, yarrow as a first aid remedy would immediately be at hand in case of injury.

Does yarrow call the fairies? Or do the fairies call forth yarrow? Many writers have explored the relationship between fairies and the natural world, particularly with flowers. Cecily Mary Barker's (1895-1973) imaginative illustrations certainly bear this out, as does a poem by Edith Nesbit (1858-1924). Her children's poem "To a Child," written in rhyming couplets, depicts

Alicia M

the miraculous world of good fairies and their ability to heal us and our world while we sleep.

The fairies have been busy while you slept;
They have been laughing where the sad rain wept,
They have taught Beauty to the ignorant flowers,
Set tasks of hope to weary wind-torn bowers,
And heard the lessons learned in school-rooms cold
By seedling snapdragon and marigold.
At dawn, while still you slept, I grew aware
How good the fairies are, how many and fair.

Nesbit's poem traces a year of flowers kept beautifully by the fairies that live unseen in our gardens. Each fairy is dressed in a different color, symbolic of the season's flowery hues. At night, for example, the golden fairy flits around the garden, lighting up yellow flowers from spring to fall, symbolic of riches, sunshine, and beauty:

Then she whose gown is gold, and gold her hair,
Swept down the golden steep straight sunbeam-stair,

She lit the tulip-lamps, she lit the torch
Of hollyhock beside the cottage porch.
She dressed the honeysuckle in fringe of gold,
She gave the king-cups fairy wealth to hold,
She kissed St. John's wort till it opened wide,
She set the yarrow by the river side …

The golden fairy touched your dreams, my child.

For me, nothing says *herb garden* like a stand of yellow yarrow resplendent in the sunshine. Yellow yarrow—here probably *A. filipendulina*, an Asian variety that blooms both summer and fall, with gray-green foliage and sturdy stems—adds its glorious yellow-gold hues to the story. Contemporary hybrids are touted as pollinator-friendly, drought-tolerant once established, beneficial to insects, attractive to butterflies, deer and rabbit resistant, with lovely cut flowers, or, if left on plants, of much winter interest, particularly in snowy areas. As an ornamental, yellow yarrow is reliable and easy to grow—especially if you have fairies in the garden—it spreads without being invasive and offers a perennial drift of color. The flowers look great in bouquets and arrangements and dry especially well.

Here's to the 2024 Herb of the Year™

Whether field-grown or garden-cultivated, this lovely wildflower has taken on various meanings and symbolic associations throughout history. Yarrow has been a revered herb wherever it is found, with strong beliefs in its power to heal and protect and celebrated for its beauty in the gardens and fields.

Sun-loving yarrow thrives in dry meadows, along roadsides, even lawns (it can take mowing), and will edge into your formal gardens if you let it. All of these locations are its rightful place. With its many attributes, yarrow, as the Herb of the Year™ 2024, belongs in children's, fairy, healing, literary, magical, ornamental, perennial, and pollinator gardens—in fact almost every themed garden.

References

Bennett, Robin Rose. *The Gift of Healing Herbs*. North Atlantic Books, 2014.

Cunningham, Scott. *Cunningham's Encyclopedia of Magical Herbs*. Llewellyn, 1994.

---*Magical Herbalism*. Llewellyn, 1995.

Dawson, Adele G. *Health, Happiness and the Pursuit of Herbs*. Stephen Greene Press, 1980. 210-212.

Dugan, Ellen. *Cottage Witchery: Natural Magick for Hearth and Home*. Llewellyn, 2008.

Dunwich, Gerina. *Magick Potions*. Citadel Press, 1998.

Emerson, Ralph Waldo. "Nature." *The Norton Book of Nature Writing*, eds Finch, Robert and John Elder. W.W. Norton & Co., 2002. 141.

Fazio, Lisa. "Italian Folk Medicine." Plant Cunning Conference, 9/9/23.

Forsell, Mary. *Heirloom Herbs: Using Old-Fashioned Herbs in Gardens, Recipes and Decorations*. Villard Books, 1990.

Forti, John. *The Heirloom Gardener: Traditional Plants & Skills for the Modern World*. Timber Press, 2021. 238.

Grieve, Maude. *A Modern Herbal*. Barnes & Noble, 1996 (1931).

Heinerman, John. *Heinerman's Encyclopedia of Juices, Teas & Tonics*. Prentice Hall, 1996. 188.

Herbs: 1001 Gardening Questions Answered. Garden Way Publ., 1990.

Huson, Paul. *Herbalism: A Practical Guide*. Stein & Day, 1974.

Kowalchik, Claire and William H. Hylton, eds. *Rodale's Illustrated Encyclopedia of Herbs*. Rodale Press, 1987. 516-519.

Longfellow, Henry Wadsworth. "Hiawatha's Lament." *Poetry.com*. www.poetry.com/poem-analysis/18627/hiawatha%27s-lamentation. Accessed 7/15/23.

Lust, John. *The Herb Book*. Bantam, 1974.

McIntyre, Anne. *Flower Power: Flower Remedies for Healing Body and Soul Through Herbalism, Homeopathy, and Aromatherapy*. Henry Holt & Co., 1996.

Morrison, Dorothy. *Bud, Blossom & Leaf: The Magical Herb Gardener's Handbook*. Llewellyn, 2001.

Nesbit, Edith. "To a Child." *Poetry.com*. STANDS4 LLC, 2023. Web. 15 Aug. 2023. www.poetry.com/poem-analysis/9031/to-a-child. Accessed 8/15/2023.

Rago, Linda Ours. *Mugworts in May: a folklore of herbs*. Quarter Press, 1995.

Reader's Digest's The Magic and Medicine of Plants. Reader's Digest Assoc., 1986.

Robinson, Edwin Arlington. "Pasa Thalassa Thalassa." EDWIN ARLINGTON ROBINSON: A Virtual Tour of Robinson's Gardiner, Maine. www.earobinson.com/pages/sites/site12.html. Accessed 8/15/2023.

Sanders, Jack. *Hedgemaids and Fairy Candles*. Ragged Mountain Press, 1993. 135-136.

Silverman, Maida. *A City Herbal*. Knopf, 1997. 163-168.

Simmons, Adelma Grenier. *A Witch's Brew*. Clinton Press, n.d.

"Spearmint: Health Benefits and More." *MedicalNewsToday*. July 23, 2023. www.medicalnewstoday.com/articles/266128. Accessed 8/15/2023.

Still, Cecil C. *Botany and Healing: Medicinal Plants of New Jersey and the Region*. Rutgers UP, 1998. 62-63.

Swift, Katja. "A Formula for Aid Workers." *Herbstalk*, 5/24/2017. www.herbstalk.org/blog/a-formula-for-aid-workers. Accessed 8/1/2023.

Toll, Maia. *The Illustrated Herbiary*. Storey, 2018.

Ward, Bobby J. *A Contemplation Upon Flowers: Garden Plants in Myth & Literature*. Timber Press, 2005.

Waterman, Catharine H. *Flora's Lexicon: The Language of Flowers*. Algrove Publ, 2001 (1860). 230.

Gert Coleman loves, grows, eats, and reads avidly about herbs. Retired Associate Professor of English at Middlesex County College in New Jersey, she lives on 106 acres in Middlefield, New York, where she and her husband grow herbs, flowers, trees, and at-risk native plants. As a naturalist, she developed and taught parent-tot nature programs at Staten Island Zoo and local parks, introducing children and parents to local plants, animals, and geology. In addition, she completed a medicinal herbal apprenticeship with herbalist Rosemary Gladstar.

Past president of the SI Herb Society, she helped to maintain a 70' x 70' colonial herb garden for 3 decades. For 13 years, she served as board member of the International Herb Association (IHA), and their newsletter editor for 7 years. In addition, she edited five IHA Herb of the Year™ books (*Cilantro & Coriander; Hops: Brewing and Beyond; Agastache: Anise Hyssop, Hummingbird Mints and More*; *Rubus;* and *Parsley*), and frequently writes about the legends, lore, and poetry of herbs.

She is a member of the American Botanical Council, American Herbalists Guild, Herb Society of America, United Plants Savers, and the North East Herb Association. She frequently lectures on various aspects of herbs and teaches workshops on nature writing in the wild places of New York and beyond. gertc3456@gmail.com

The silvery gray colors of white yarrow make it ornamental as well as medicinal. *Susan Belsinger*

Achillea millefolium. 224

The Harrowing
Escapades of Yarrow
Achillea millefolium

Rosemary Roman Davis

The Year is 1516 C.E.

In Europe, explorers have set forth for new destinations in Central and South America. Charles of Ghent has just ascended the throne of Spain. The Ottoman Empire has declared war upon the Mamluk Sultanate in Egypt; the Treaty of Brussels has established peace between France and the Holy Roman Empire. Italian sailors have landed on the southern shores of China, seeking trade with the merchants of the fabled Ming Dynasty.

And in Bavaria, Duke Wilhelm IV has just enacted the *Rheinheitsgebot*—the German Purity Law, one of the first substance control laws on record—which involves our protagonist, Eurasian native *Achillea millefolium.*

For millennia, cultures who utilized fermentation in their foodways and medicinal traditions knew and loved yarrow. Yarrow flourishes all over the globe in all but the most arid and desolate deserts. It is drought tolerant, laughs at poor soil, and thrives even in cold climates. It can be eaten, used medicinally and as an ingredient in plant and/or grain ferments.

Hence our sixteenth-century drama: yarrow, along with many other astringent, tonic, psychotropic and nourishing herbs, was once a key ingredient in beers and ales made throughout Europe. However, a year before Martin Luther nailed his 95 theses to the door of Wittenberg's church, setting off the fireworks of the Protestant Reformation, the battle which had been brewing (pun intended) over beer for hundreds of years was publicly ended.

Specifically, the furor revolved around who could make beer, what ingredients it could contain, who could sell it, how inebriating it could be, and who could tax it. Naturally, regulating such a common staple sparked a bitter war among the powers of church, state, and the common citizenry, which dragged out for decades before another herb nominally won the beer war due to the Rheinheitsgebot: hops. All herbs other than hops were relegated to life sentences outside of the brewer's vat, regarded as dangerous, impure, potentially intoxicating, aphrodisiac, and freely available by the side of the road (read: not taxable).

The details of the beer battle shall wait for a hop-related story, as our focus is yarrow. And yarrow has a colorful profile of which its role in brewing is only one part.

Yarrow, in the Asteraceae family (sometimes also listed as a member of the Compositae), has many common names:

Latin: *Achillea millefolium, Herba militaris, Achillea ligusticum* ("to bind with yarrow")

United Kingdom and United States: Thousand-seal, Old Man's Pepper, Sanguinary, Bloodwort, Soldier's Woundwort (this last in use during the United States' Civil War), Bad Man's Plaything

Scandinavia: *Jordhumle,* "Field hop," "earth hop"

Jutland: *Gjedebrygger,* "goat brewer"

Norway: *Hardhaus,* "hardhead"

China: *Shī*

Dakota Native American: *Tao-pi pezu'ta,* "medicine for the wounded"

Spain: *Milenrama*

Italy: *Il millefoglie*

Irish: *Athair thalun*

Gaelic: *Earr-thalmhainn* or *Lus chasgadh na fala*

The English name "yarrow" is thought to have evolved from Old English *gear(e)we,* a place name signifying land overgrown with yarrow, or Welsh *garw,* meaning "rough." Confusingly, the meaning is sometimes also given as "to treat or make healthy." There are rivers named "Yarrow" in both England and Scotland.

If we turn further back through history to our early ancestors, the presence and use of yarrow are first documented in 60,000-year-old plant remains found within a Neanderthal grave in Iraq, according to Stephen Harrod Buhner. The Maya burned yarrow on their temple altars as an offering and perhaps as a protective herb. Probably the most well-known anecdote regarding yarrow and the root of its nomenclature is found in Homer's *Iliad*, in which Chiron, the famous centaur and healer, gifts the plant to Achilles for treatment of his soldiers during the Trojan War. It is also said that yarrow infused the waters of the River Styx, in which Achilles was dipped at birth; yarrow was believed to confer immortality on those who bathed with it. (Just remember to submerge completely.)

Dioscorides wrote of yarrow's use for wound care by the Roman legions, and the Druids were known to use the herb for divinatory purposes, as were the Chinese—by casting the dried stalks similarly to casting runes, or the latter-day coins of the *I Ching*.

We know that American colonists brought the herb with them from Europe, but it is almost certain that they carried their own cultivars; many Native American tribes across North America were already using yarrow, burned for ritual purposes by shamans and healers. As in Europe, the Native Americans had also discovered its healing power for wound care, fever, indigestion, burns, gynecological complaints, earache, and toothache; a decoction of the root was used for wasting of muscle tissue. It was also considered to be an aphrodisiac.

Linnaeus reported that in Norway, yarrow tea was recommended for rheumatism and gout. Herbalists Nicholas Culpeper and John Gerard did not neglect yarrow: Culpeper calls upon it for relief of venereal diseases (since he ascribes the herb to the rule of Venus, following the ancient Greeks), incontinence, bleeding wounds, ulcers, and hemorrhoids. Gerard cites it as effective for "swellings of the privie parts."

Although when we think of yarrow we recall most often its styptic qualities, herbal lore frequently produces conflicting advice—directing the application of crushed yarrow up one's nose to either halt bleeding, or *cause* bleeding, i.e., in the desire to aid a migraine headache. (It is thought that the tiny hairs on the leaves of yarrow would provoke bleeding as a mechanical reaction in the nasal passages.) This procedure is also on yarrow's list of divinatory aspects, as putting yarrow up the nose—or simply smelling the flower head—while reciting various rhymes was believed to predict whether the object of a love-struck person's affections returned the sentiment. If your nose bled, that

Drying Yarrow. *Gail Wood Miller*

is. What all this meant—if you already had a migraine but were unlucky in love, for instance—is unclear from historical records.

It seems simpler to follow the European country girls' belief that sleeping with yarrow under your pillow—yarrow cut before sunrise, mind you—would produce a dream of your true love. Unfortunately, if his back was turned to you in the dream, it signified the dreamer's love would be spurned. If facing the dreamer, marriage lay in the future. If the divination proved accurate, the bride was advised to carry yarrow in her wedding bouquet to ensure seven happy years.

Yarrow's folkloric reputation, as with many other bitter herbs, is strongly linked with protection against evil as well as disease. In northern Europe it was specifically dedicated to the goddess Freya, appropriate as she is the Norse goddess of love, fertility, battle and death. Yarrow can be eaten, although chopping it into a salad guarantees a definitely bitter dining experience unless used sparingly.

"Old man's pepper" refers not only to yarrow's historical use as a seasoning but also as an ingredient in snuff. (Whether the snuff prevented or caused nosebleeds, and what the romantic prospects of the old men were, is also not well documented.) "Bad man's plaything" may be related to its use applied to contusions—yarrow being the herb you grab from the roadside on the way home for your black eye, received in a rowdy brawl at the pub!

In other practical uses, yarrow is indeed much more than just a styptic. It is anti-inflammatory, a febrifuge, an emmenagogue, hepatic, mildly sedative when ingested, astringent, tonic, analgesic, antispasmodic, digestive, diaphoretic, diuretic, anticatarrhal, and antiseptic.

The active chemical components in yarrow are many and versatile, according to Michael Castleman:

Achilletin and achilleine glycoalkaloids (coagulant/hemostatic)

Azulene, eugenol, menthol, quercetin, rutin, terpeniol, tannins, and salicylic acid (analgesic and antiseptic)

Chamazulene (digestive and antispasmodic)

Flavonoids and coumarins (bittering agents)

Thujone (mild hypnotic)

The trace amount of thujone in yarrow brings us back to the beer wars of the sixteenth century, and the arguments over using mildly or strongly psychotropic plants in brewing. Many common herbs besides yarrow contain trace amounts of what we today class as controlled substances, especially when acting in combination with alcohol.

The legislation which resulted in hops being the only approved herbal ingredient in beer was presented to the European public as a safety measure, since hops are an effective preservative. But many other psychoactive plants, including yarrow, act as bittering and preservative agents. Hops, it must be noted, are sedative, while many other psychotropic plants are not. Public health issue, or regulatory interference? The reader must judge for him- or herself. Even as a tea or bath herb, yarrow used on its own has the reputation of aiding psychic abilities and heightening spiritual awareness. In the Hebrides the tea applied as an eye poultice was thought to enhance the Second Sight.

Some persons with a sensitivity to ragweed may develop a rash or mild photosensitivity if using yarrow externally, but in general it is harmless used in an infusion as a skin wash, hair rinse (said to combat baldness and scalp irritation), as a compress or poultice, tincture, tea, or ferment. Both the root and the leaves are used. For best efficacy the plant should be harvested when flowering, from June to September in most temperate climes. As with many herbs, yarrow is best avoided during pregnancy.

Yarrow's simplest first-aid use is to crush (or chew) a few of the leafy fronds and tape the plant matter on a bleeding cut, shaving scrape, or bug bite with an adhesive strip. When you do this, remember that we were still calling upon yarrow as a readily available wound dressing during the First World War.

For face washes (especially helpful for oily or acne-prone skin), boil a heaping cup of yarrow foliage, preferably fresh, in two cups of distilled or spring water for ten minutes. Let cool, strain, and use as a face rinse—or add a few drops of castile soap to make a mild astringent facewash. Use the plain tea undiluted as a hair rinse. Make a fresh infusion every two to three days for ongoing use. If fresh foliage is not available, dried leaves may be substituted.

Internally, the tea has been used for arthritis, gout, urinary tract infections, hyperthyroidism, colds and flu, fevers, water retention, and high blood pressure.

Yarrow essential oil is commercially available but should be used with caution, liberally diluted, due to its concentration. Its natural color is vivid blue due to the azulene compounds in the raw plant. No essential oil should ever be used internally, and most essential oils should be avoided if pregnant or breastfeeding.

Yarrow seen in the wild (in USDA Zones 2 to 9) favors sunny areas, often with poor and dry soil. Wild yarrow is usually creamy white, or occasionally white with a pinkish tinge. In the garden, yarrow forms a tidy and sturdy perennial clump one to three feet high, which typically does not need support from heavy rain or wind. The tough root clumps are superlative for combatting erosion of depleted and stony soils. Modern cultivars now include bright golden yellow, soft pink, and deep magenta varieties along with the familiar white. Depending on the mordant used, yarrow foliage will produce a pale green or yellow fabric dye.

For medicinal purposes, wild yarrow is usually recommended over the domesticated versions, although modern yarrow can certainly be used. When clumps in the garden grow large, it is advisable to divide yarrow in the spring or fall, at least every three to four years, to maintain its health; otherwise the center of the clump will die out and leave the gardener with an unattractive sprawling mess.

Outside the house, yarrow is a powerful compost activator and it is said that only a few sprays added to a compost pile promote excellent decomposition. In animal husbandry, the dried herb is used as fodder in Northern Europe, and sheep in particular will seek it out as both a food and a tonic.

For human culinary use, yarrow is best used sparingly due to its strong flavor, which has been compared to anise and tarragon, but is to my palate a completely different take on "bittersweet".

Some sources have reported enjoying yarrow boiled as a green vegetable and buttered, but I tend to lean toward using the fresh herb or the flowers, sparingly, chopped into a salad or tossed with a pasta featuring a rich tomato sauce or sausage. A sprig or two minced into your salsa or gazpacho would not go amiss.

Here are some suggestions for your next adventure with yarrow:

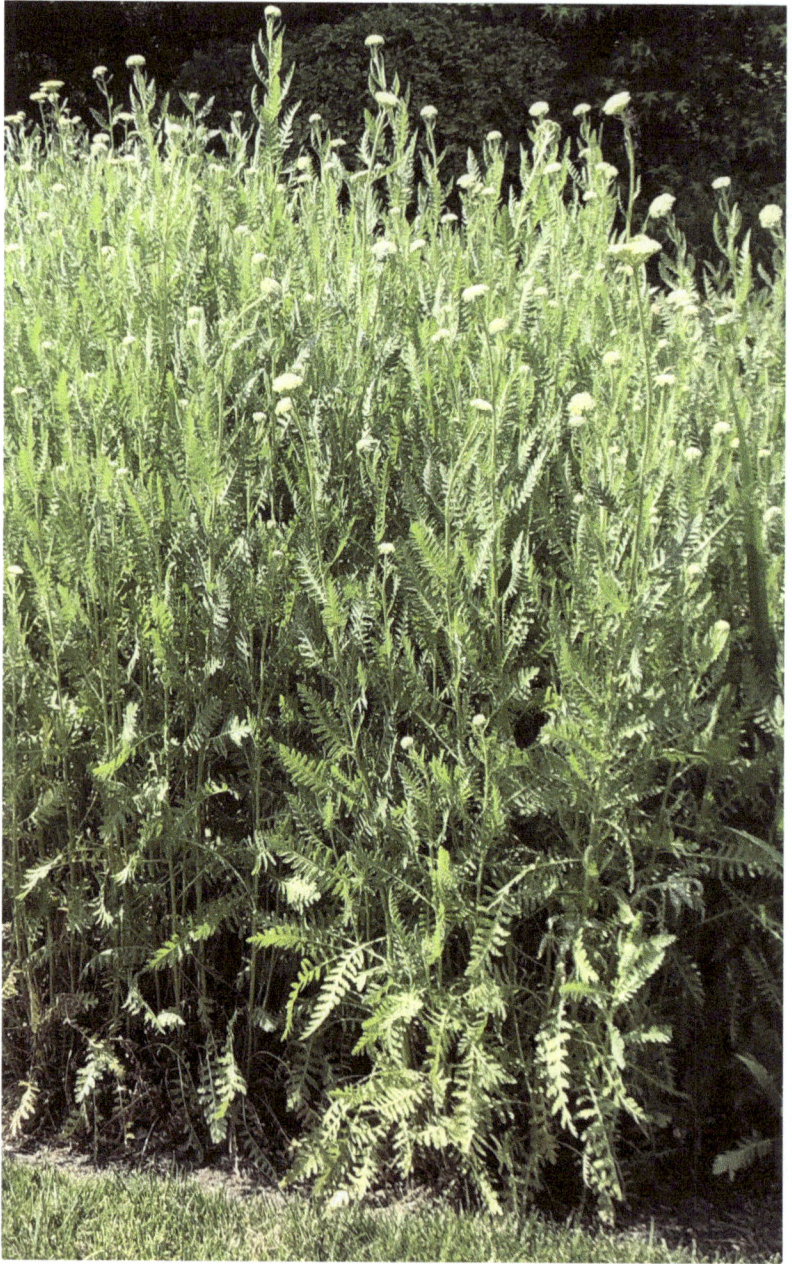

Yarrow is a plant that takes hold and spreads easily in the garden. The bitter taste of the leaves and flowers deters wildlife from eating it. *Susan Belsinger*

Homemade Bitters

This simple method for home-made bitters has served my family well for decades. Please note that other herbs, plants and seeds in addition to yarrow can and should be used in your bitters for their tonic and digestive qualities, depending on your desired flavor profile. Yarrow alone in bitters would be a bit much!

Think of balancing your bitter herbs such as yarrow, dandelion, hops, or mugwort with a little sweetness (from fruit or flowers), and perhaps a seed or spice. Your home-made bitters are not going to be as intense as those you buy in the store; commercial bitters often contain ingredients you won't find in your local market.

For yarrow, both the leaves and root can be used in bitters. Be aware that using the root will be more intensely bitter in your finished product than foliage used alone.

I personally like to add citrus zest, ginger, edible flowers such as rose, lavender, or hibiscus, and aromatic seeds such as cardamom, coriander, fenugreek, and fennel to my blends. Experiment with different small batches and remember to label which batch is which, so you can duplicate your favorites!

Measurements here are not exact, and do not need to be, but when beginning to experiment, use a rough ratio of 6 ounces herb/fruit/spice material to 1 cup of alcohol. Expand this to fit the size of your steeping vessel as needed.

Stuff a glass or ceramic jar—think a jam jar or Mason jar to start—with your yarrow and other plant matter, spices if using, and some seasonal fruit such as cherries, plums, blackberries or blueberries. Leave the pits in if using stone fruit. The ingredients can be sliced or crushed to fit your container, but precise chopping is not necessary.

Fill the jar completely with high-proof vodka and poke the organic material with a chopstick or skewer to release all air bubbles. Steep this in a cool dark place for two to three weeks. Shake the jar at least every few days. Use smell and taste to monitor how strong the solution has become. If in doubt, leave it to steep longer, or strain out some of your solids and replace half of them with fresh material to intensify flavor for another week or so.

When you are satisfied with the infusion, strain out the solids, set the vodka aside, and put the organic material in a saucepan with enough water to almost cover. Simmer for 15 minutes. Turn off the heat, cover the pan, and let the organic material steep overnight.

The next day, strain out the solids and compost them if possible. To the remaining liquid, add 2 to 3 tablespoons of sugar depending on your amount of liquid—add the sugar one tablespoon at a time, warm or stir until dissolved, and taste after each addition. The solution should be sweet but not overly so.

Combine with the infused alcohol, transfer to a clean container, (label and date!) and shake well before each use. Consume straight as a digestive (a small shot in some soda water) or in the botanical cocktail of your choice.

Chiron's Rescue Salve

I am sure Achilles had a jar of this stashed somewhere in his chariot. Excellent for cuts, scrapes, bug bites, dry feet, gardener's hands, and minor Trojan War injuries. Recommended for rough heels after your dip in the Styx.

Yield: about 1/4 cup

First, make the yarrow-infused oil:
3/4 cup extra-virgin olive oil (or more, as needed)
1 heaping cupful of chopped fresh yarrow leaves and flowers

Place chopped yarrow in double boiler pan with olive oil, making sure the herbs are covered. Infuse the herbs over very low heat for several hours, until the plant matter is absolutely wilted. Turn off heat and let steep overnight.

Squash the herbs with a potato masher or fork the next day to get out every bit of goodness.

Strain the infused oil.

To make the salve:
Yarrow infused olive oil
5 tablespoons grated or pelletized beeswax (I prefer pelletized)
1 tablespoon liquid lanolin
1 tablespoon coconut oil

1 tablespoon raw honey
1/8 teaspoon baking soda
10 drops essential oil of your choice (lavender, tea tree, rosemary, frankincense, helichrysum, and peppermint are all good options—feel free to mix and match.)

In a double boiler melt the beeswax, lanolin, coconut oil, honey and baking soda (everything except the essential oils) in the herb-infused oil over very low heat; stir until all are blended; let cool slightly. Add the essential oils when the oil reaches room temperature; pour the mixture into a small container. Stir and let cool completely.

Please note that in un-air-conditioned areas or hot weather, your salve will be thinner; in cold weather it will be more solid, closer to a salve. If it is summer and you feel your salve is too liquid, melt in a little more beeswax and re-pour into your container to make firmer. Or simply keep your salve in the fridge.

Yarrow has been a firm friend to humankind for many a year. Easy to grow, uniquely fragrant, reliably perennial, and endlessly helpful, it is hoped that you will make room in your garden and your pantry for this attractive and distinctive plant.

Happy Gardening and Blessed Be!

References

Balch, James F., M.D. and Stengler, Mark, M.D. *Prescription for Natural Cures*. John Wiley & Sons, Inc., 2004.

Beith, Mary. *Healing Threads: Traditional Medicines of the Highlands and Islands.* Polygon, 1995.

Bremness, Lesley. *Herbs.* DK Publishing, Inc., 1994.

Buhner, Stephen Harrod. *Sacred and Herbal Healing Beers: The Secrets of Ancient Fermentation.* Siris Books, 1998.

Castleman, Michael. *The Healing Herbs.* Rodale Press, 1991.

Cox, Janice. *Natural Beauty for All Seasons.* Henry Holt and Company, Inc., 1996.

de Baïracli Levy, Juliette. *The Complete Herbal Handbook for Farm and Stable.* Faber and Faber Ltd., 1991.

Duke, James A., Ph.D. *A Field Guide to Medicinal Plants: Eastern and Central North America.* Rodale Press, 1987.

--- . *The Green Pharmacy.* Rodale Press, 1997.

Gerard, John. *The Herball or Generall Historie of Plantes.* London, United Kingdom: John Norton, 1597.

Grieve, Mrs. Maud. *A Modern Herbal in Two Volumes*; Vol. II: I-Z. Dover Publications, 1971.

Hoffman, David. *The New Holistic Herbal.* Element Books, Inc., 1992.

Jackson, Mildred, N.D. and Teague, Terri, N.D. *The Handbook of Alternatives to Chemical Medicine.* Coconino County, 1975.

Keville, Kathi. *Herbs: An Illustrated Encyclopedia.* Michael Friedman Publishing, Inc., 1994.

McIntyre, Anne. *The Medicinal Garden.* Henry Holt and Company, Inc., 1997.

Neal, Bill. *Gardener's Latin.* Algonquin Books, 1992.

Personal notes, *Proceedings of the International Herb Symposium*, Norton, MA, 2000-2013.

Pond, Barbara. *A Sampler of Wayside Herbs.* Greenwich House, 1974.

Rose, Jeanne. *The Herbal Body Book.* Perigee Books, 1976.

---. 375 *Essential Oils and Hydrosols.* Frog, Ltd., 1999.

Seymour, Miranda. *A Brief History of Thyme and other herbs.* Grove Press, 2002.

Stewart, Amy. *Wicked Plants: The Weed That Killed Lincoln's Mother & Other Botanical Atrocities.* Algonquin Books of Chapel Hill, 2009.

Tiwari, Maya. *Ayurveda: A Life of Balance.* Healing Arts Press, 1995.

Tourles, Stephanie. *The Herbal Body Book: A Natural Approach to Healthier Hair, Skin and Nails.* Storey Communications, Inc., 1995.

Zachos, Ellen. *The Wildcrafted Cocktail.* Storey Publishing, 2017.

Rosemary Roman Davis was raised in a family of herbalists and green thumbs, and maintains a messy but vibrant organic garden in upstate New York. When not finding new excuses to avoid weeding and planning for the next big endeavor—beekeeping—she is a licensed massage therapist and Reiki Master. She has also been an adult education teacher for over fifteen years, offering food folklore classes and many hands-on workshops including soapmaking, cheesemaking and papermaking.

The Education of Achilles, Jean-Baptiste Regnault, 1782. www.wikimediacommons.com

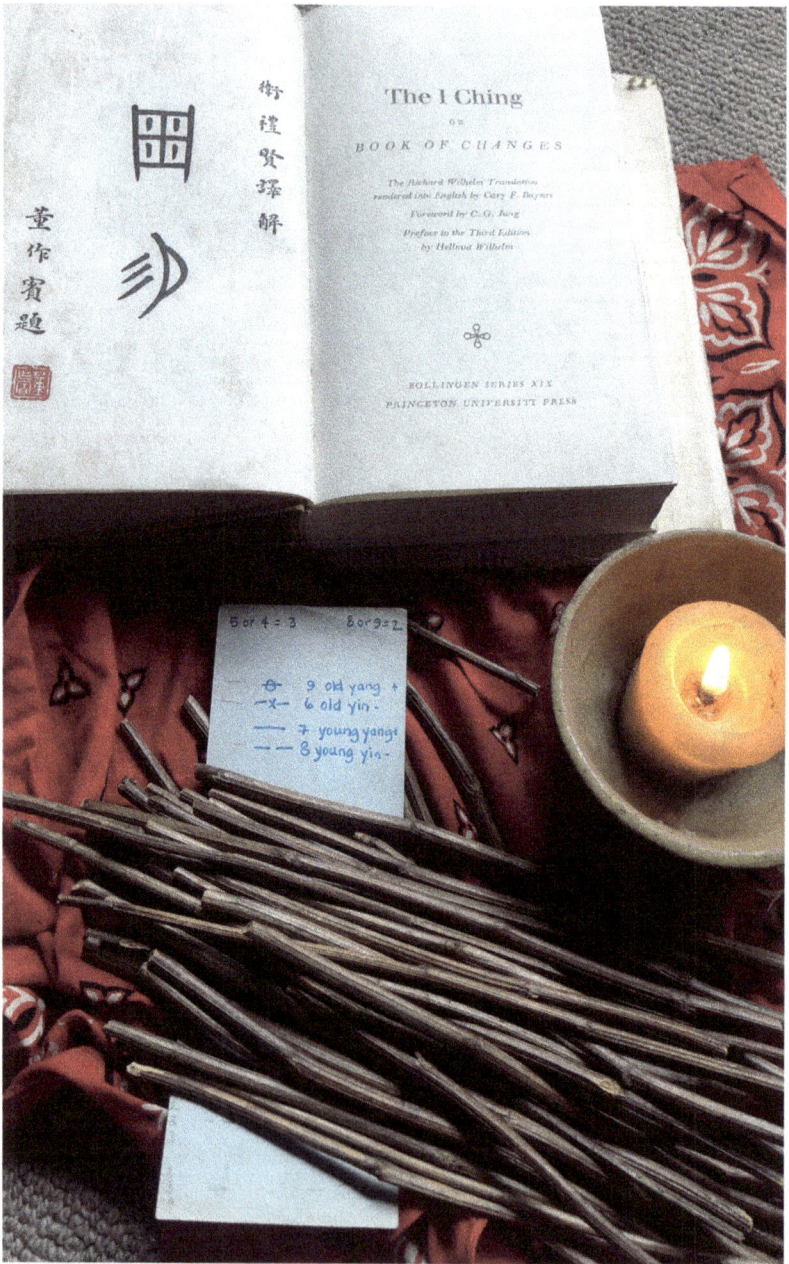

Yarrow stalks are used in the oracle of the *I Ching*. *Susan Belsinger*

My Introduction to Using Yarrow Stalks and the *I Ching*

Susan Belsinger

In 1972, I was living in Verona, Italy and the Marseglia family whom I was staying with decided to go to Tuscany over Easter vacation. We stayed in an old stone Tuscan farmhouse in a hill town called Vaglia (pronounced vahl-yah) about 18 to 20 kilometers north of Firenze. During our time there, we heard of an artists' commune in the neighborhood, where there were Italians and Americans living and working, so we went to visit Studio Acquirico.

It was there I met Carolyn Dille, a Californian living in Italy, and we hit it off immediately. We spent a few days hanging out in the art studio (they did commercial silk screening), listening to music, cooking, firing up the stone oven to bake bread and spending time in the garden. There was yarrow in the herb garden and Carolyn showed me the *I Ching,* also known as *Book of Changes,* and how to "throw the yarrow stalks" and interpret this ancient Chinese oracle.

We spent an afternoon cutting yarrow stalks so I could have my own set and we made another set for Studio Acquirico. There are 50 stalks in a set, so we cut long stalks which were about three feet tall, trimmed off the flowers and stripped the leaves to dry for tea and then cut the stalks into about 9- to 10-inch lengths. I was so delighted to have them and I wrapped them in a red bandana that I had in my backpack and tied them with a scrap of leather cord. Since then, those yarrow stalks have traveled with me near and far and I have recorded every date and time that I have used them on bookmarks, ticket stubs and assorted pieces of paper which are folded into the back pages of my *Book of Changes.*

I savor the ceremony of casting my stalks and interpreting the hexagrams; I usually light a candle before I begin. First, I unroll the bandana and hold the stalks to set my intent or ask my question and sit quietly with them. Then I place the stalks on the bandana and begin the process of counting them and placing them between my fingers and then laying them out into neat piles, just as Carolyn showed me how to do it. (This procedure is given in detail in the introduction of the *I Ching*; however I think it is much more pleasurable to have someone show you how to do it, than to read the process and figure it out.)

One of the times that I was returning to the U.S. from Europe, they searched my backpack at customs. They seized my bundle of yarrow stalks, my bulb of garlic, an imported chocolate bar and a little bag of white toothpowder (salt and potassium alum for brushing teeth), telling me that I could not bring plant material or food into the country. Well, I had a good long wait while they analyzed the tooth powder, and so I explained (somewhat tearfully) to the officials that the yarrow was long dried and had been back and forth across the ocean more than once, and that they were precious to me. Bottom line, I got the yarrow stalks back as well as the toothpowder—they kept the garlic bulb—and I never saw my dark chocolate with hazelnuts again.

The yarrow stalks are now over 50 years old and well worn. As you can see from the photo—they are still mostly intact. The bandana hasn't fared as well—it has holes—I suppose I should wrap them in a new one, however I have a sentimental attachment to the old one. The book is also worn and the cloth cover is somewhat discolored; the paper cover is long gone. I have a set of three antique Chinese coins, which can also be used with the book of oracles, however I only used them once. I much prefer the feel of the yarrow stalks between my fingers and the sound of them clicking together as they are stacked, while performing this age-old ritual.

The copy of the *I Ching or Book of Changes* that I use is *The Richard Wilhelm Translation rendered into English by Cary F. Baynes* edition, Bollingen series XIX, Princeton University Press, 1970.

Susan Belsinger bio on page 11

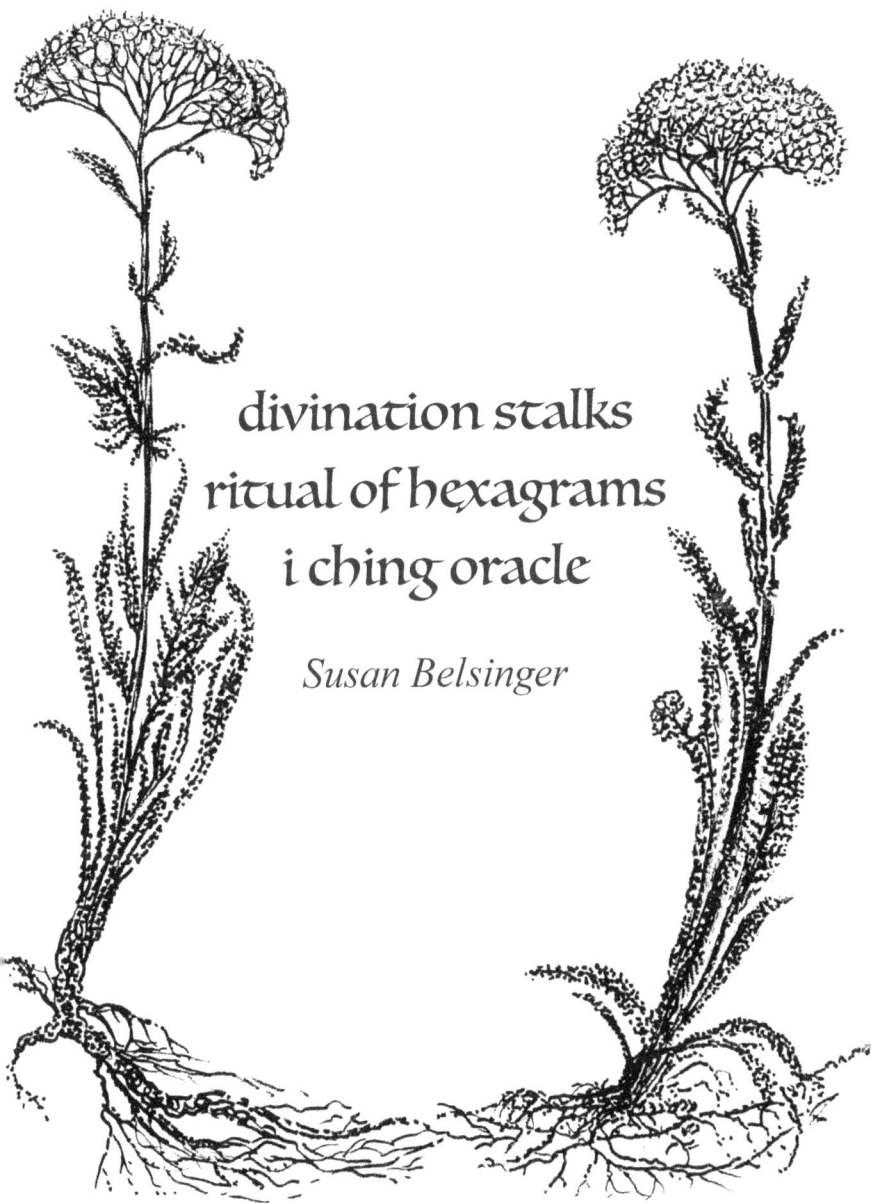

divination stalks
ritual of hexagrams
i ching oracle

Susan Belsinger

Downward look into hollowness of cut yarrow stalks. *Pat Kenny*

Yarrow, or Milfoil, as Aid with *I Ching* Study

Pat Kenny

"Sometimes one can give nature a little push, if one knows the art of it, but it must be a push very nearly in the direction things are going anyway. There are some who know to value teaching without words, to cultivate the art of leaving well enough alone. Attuned to nature's rhythms effort is conserved and energy reserved within for application when appropriate: the proper action, in the right place at the most opportune moment – correctly responsive to the situation" ---*Taoism*, Blofeld, p. 195.

The strong, rounded, straight hollow stalks of *Achillea* (*millefolium* or *sibirica*) have been traditionally used with the *I Ching* (pronounced Yee Jing), the *Book of Changes*, an ancient text of wisdom, one of the Six Classics of Confucian study.[1,2]

Their upright growth symbolizes the human being's natural orientation and mode of movement connecting the heavens and our planet Earth with the Universe: Heaven—Earth—and Humankind. Looking at the order of the firmament above, it is said that ancient peoples have tried to re-enact that order on Earth. Since the yarrow plant was found to lend itself to so many medicinal uses, it came to be considered as a spiritual source as well. Its common occurrence over the lands made it easily obtainable long before metallurgy and the minting of coins. Coins are used nowadays as a short-cut method of consulting the *I Ching*.

One of the oldest procedures calls for fifty yarrow stalks selected in the late afternoon during the autumnal season, well after blooming from peaceful unpolluted sunny places and each cut one to two feet long.

To use yarrow stalks to "throw" the *I Ching*, set one stalk aside, which symbolizes the all-encompassing Unknown Infinity. As instructed in the *Book of Changes*, the hands make random divisions of the forty-nine stalks.

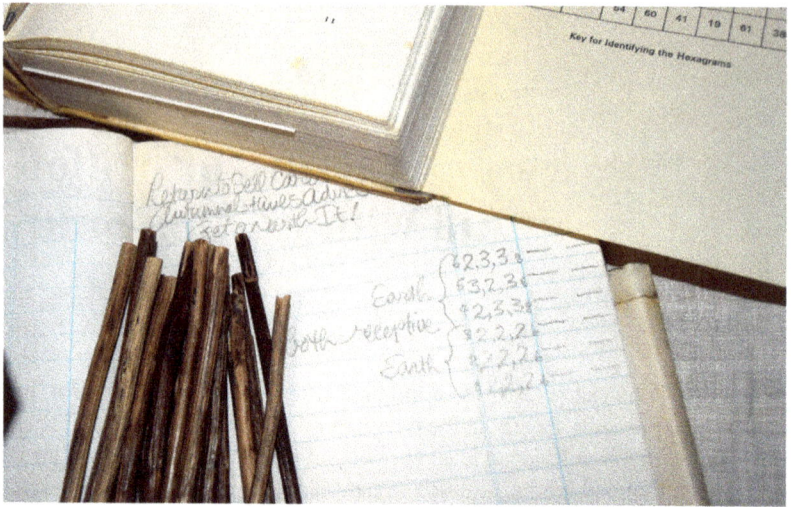

A grouping of sticks and a beginning notation of a hexagram. *Pat Kenny*

This is done by counting repeated stalk divisions, three per line, and totaling them with designated numerical symbols. A six-lined figure (hexagram) is constructed from these numbers, which is read from the bottom up. It is an exacting process which can take about thirty minutes away from the usual hurried, superficial daily routine. For this reason and that of its being an organic link with the Cosmos, the yarrow stalk method is preferred to that of dropping three coins on a flat surface six times.

Among others, the translations of the *I Ching* by Wilhelm/Baynes, pp.721-724, and Wu Jing-Nuan, pp. 46-48, include descriptions of the Yarrow Stalk Method. Because it is not easy to describe a dynamic procedure in two dimensional images on paper, we suggest, if interested, that you tune into YouTube videos to see the practice of using the yarrow stalk method of constructing hexagrams for consulting the *I Ching*.

The consultation of the *I Ching* can be used as a basis for reflection, contemplation, meditation, as a lead for furthering a human's knowledge of him or herself and the Universe, and for practical guidance on the everyday problems of life: health, relationships, business, politics, travel and social events. "Basic ideas in the book were probably handed down from the elders of the nomadic tribes of Siberia observing the stars, tides, plants, animals, and cycles of all natural events. It was most widely used as a farming, fishing, and hunting almanac, until King Wen wrote essays on the meanings of the sixty-four hexagrams—six-lined figures which each represent a particular human situation in life. The accompanying English translation of the ancient text tells how one may best behave within it."[3]

It is thought that as life changes, we apparently move at random through the patterns of the *I Ching*. If we know where we are at any given time, we could receive instructions as to what our condition is and how to conduct ourselves with wisdom and virtue amid those particular circumstances. "Think of it as clicking the shutter of a camera in order to capture a picture of the moment and examine in detail the meaning."[4]

Although faddists have used the *I Ching* with superstition for fortune-telling, it does not predict or determine the future. It could be said to describe the developing edge of our current experience only as far ahead as the gap between one's experience and understanding. It can help one see those aspects of one's experience not felt clearly.[5]

"As a person matures to sageness, the explicit knowledge of the formal pronouncement of the hexagrams disappears into his deeper subconscious. Eventually, he becomes oblivious of the very preachings themselves, and the spirit of the *I Ching* merges with his very being. From then on, his actions are no longer heralded by his own learning but evoked by the universal harmony. Being one with nature, he apprehends the All-totally instantaneously, ineffably. This is the ultimate lesson of the *I Ching*." ---*The Portable Dragon*, R.G.H.Siu, pp.8-9.

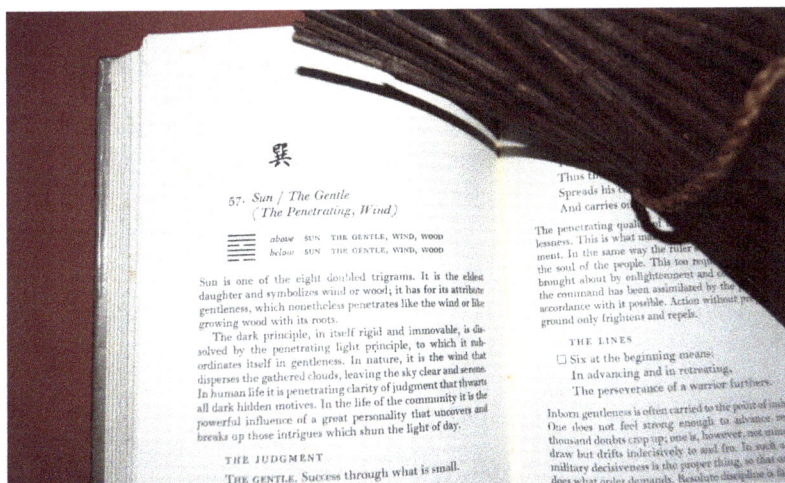

Randomly opened *I Ching* book for today, 8-30-2023. *Pat Kenny*

1. *A Sourcebook in Chinese Philosophy*. Translated and compiled by Wing-tsit Chan, Princeton University Press, 1969, 1973, p.4.
2. *An Anthology of I Ching*. W. A. Sherrill and W. K. Chu, Routledge and Kegan Paul, Henley and Boston, 1977, p.7.
3. *The I Ching Workbook*. R. L. Wing, Doubleday and Co., Inc., 1979, p. 8, para. 5.
4. Ibid, p.9, para. 3.
5. *I Ching Primer*. Frank R. Kegan, The Aries Press, 1979, p. v., para.3.

References

Blofeld, John. *Taoism, The Road to Immortality*. Shambala Publications, 1978.

Dhiegh, Khigh Alx. *The Eleventh Wing: An Exposition of the Dynamics of I Ching For Now*. Nash Publishing, 1973.

Hook, Diana ffarington. *The I Ching and You*. E.P. Dutton, 1973.

---. *The I Ching and Mankind*. Routledge and Kegan Paul, 1975.

Siu, R.G.H. *The Portable Dragon, The Western Man's Guide to the I Ching*. (original edition published under *The Man of Many Qualities*: *A Legacy of the I Ching*). MIT Press,1968.

Wilhelm, Hellmut, translated by Cary F. Baynes, Bollingen Foundation, 1960. *Eight Lectures on the I Ching*. Princeton University Press, 1973.

Wu, Jing-Nuan. *Yi Jing translated by Wu Jing-Nuan*. Asian Spirituality, Taoist Studies Series, The Taoist Center, Washington D.C., Distributed by University of Hawaii Press, 1991.

Most Widely Used Translations of *I Ching*:

The I Ching of Book of Changes, *The Richard Wilhelm translation rendered into English by Cary F. Baynes*, 1950, Bollingen Foundation, Princeton University Press, 1967, 10th printing 1973.

The I Ching, The Book of Changes, translated by James Legge, 2nd edition, Dover Publications, 1963.

I Ching: A new Interpretation for Modern Times. Sam Reifler, Bantam Books 1974.

Yi Jing translated by Wu Jing-Nuan. Asian Spirituality, Taoist Studies Series, The Taoist Center, Washington D. C., Distributed by University of Hawaii Press, 1991.

Pat Kenny: A version of this write-up was written fifty years ago; I was in my thirties and seeking advice from several angles. I was reading *Organic Gardening* and *Prevention* magazines. I was attending classes in nutrition and macrobiotics. Volunteering in a local co-op, I saw a note on the bulletin board advertising a beginning T'ai Chi class in someone's home. I had seen T'ai Chi mentioned as a moving meditation in health improvement and longevity, so I signed up.

Working as a medical illustrator at the National Institutes of Health, I found and was able to borrow my first T'ai Chi book from the National Library of Medicine. Over the years these studies led me to the *I Ching* which led me to fields of yarrow in Pennsylvania and Virginia. Many collected yarrow stalks survived the renovation and sale of the house next door; we are living in the house we used to rent.

During the years of the late 1970s and 80s, I consulted the *I Ching* somewhat regularly, making notes in journals. Because I consider the yarrow stalk ritual as an aid to self-knowledge, I usually say to myself something like the thought: "How am I doing? May these *keys* unlock the wisdom of this book so I may experience the enlightenment that comes with consciousness expansion."

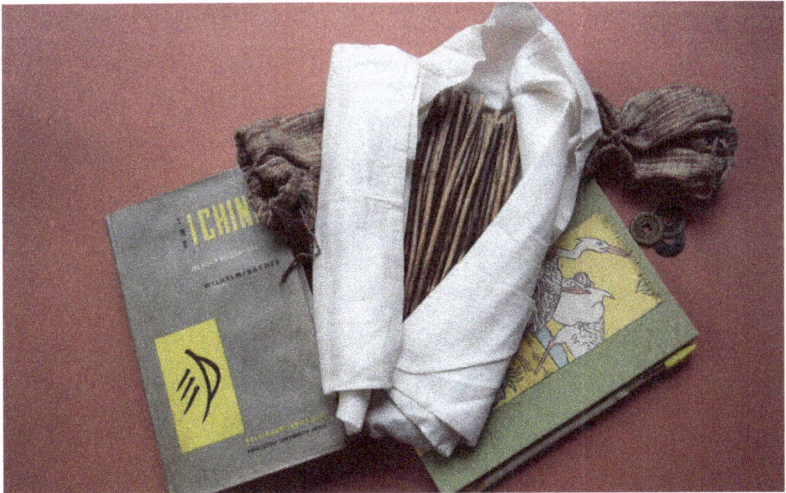

My reference copy of the *I Ching*, customized raw Chinese silk, yarrow stalk and coin cloth container, and my *I Ching* journal—stalks in one of my father's linen hankerchiefs. *Pat Kenny*

Yarrow Recipes

Pale pink yarrow blooms. *Pat Crocker*

In the Kitchen with Yarrow

Pat Crocker

My goals with this article were to search for historical proof that yarrow was used as an ingredient in recipes for the dinner table and to create new recipes for cooking with yarrow. My first step in writing about plants and food is always to take a deep dive into my library of herbals and immerse myself in the work of both ancient and modern herbalists. After all, we're all standing on the shoulders of those who sowed or foraged, harvested, cooked, made medicine, and learned from the plants growing now as they were centuries ago. It always amazes me that the same plants are still providing gifts for us.

Going into the research, I guess I held some assumptions and pre-judged yarrow, *Achillea millefolium* (*millefolium* meaning 'herb of a million leaves') as an herb known *only* for its medicine and as a somewhat showy garden flower. Rarely, I thought, do we harvest and use the herb for culinary delights. Does that mean that yarrow is only used for medicine and ornamental purposes? Have people not used yarrow as an ingredient for cooking?

While it is edible, its rather sharp, slightly bitter, astringent taste, not to mention its sudorific effect (it causes profuse sweating) have likely deterred most of us from experimenting with it in food or drink. Although, in his book, *The Chemistry of Common Life* (1879), J. Johnston writes, "The leaves of Yarrow or Milfoil have the property of producing intoxication. These are also used in the north of Sweden by the Dalecarlians[1] to give headiness to their beer." Intoxication? I stumble forward.

Almost one hundred years later, Richard Le Strange offers up encouragement to my culinary pursuit, advising that of about forty species of *Achillea* growing in Europe, only one other than *A. millefolium* is used as medicine or in drinks and food, the other being *A. ptarmica.* Quite predictably, he reports that, "the young shoots were included as a matter of course in salads 'to correct the coldness of other herbs' … " I picture lettuce and cabbage, and other greens shivering in a salad bowl and wonder if the peppery taste of yarrow sparks some kind of warming balance when tossed into their midst.

I turn next to Judith Sumner (*The Natural History of Medicinal Plants*, 2000), who notes that "Yarrow contains more than one hundred biologically active secondary compounds ... ," some of which are anti-inflammatory, hemostatic, and help treat colds, fevers, and bleeding. Alma Hutchens (*Indian Herbalogy of North America*, 1991) asserts that yarrow was known as a useful tonic for run-down conditions and in colds, influenza, measles, smallpox, chickenpox, fevers, and acute catarrhs of the respiratory tract. And of course, all this spurs me on to finding ways to include yarrow in food. Because what we eat every day should nourish, prevent illness, and keep us healthy.

Apart from this tip from Claire Loewenfeld and Philippa Back, "Natural condiments are wild garlic, horseradish, rock samphire, stonecrop, wild fennel, thyme and mint, hyssop and yarrow in place of parsley," I can find no culinary uses for yarrow. OK, I can design a not-too-cold salad and create a kickass herbal seasoning. Is that all?

I turn next to a cursory online search. Bingo! I land on Robin Harford's *Eatweeds* blog (see References, this blog is amazing!). Robin assures us that the entire plant is edible, raw or cooked. Great, now we're cooking ... or not. I've been thinking I'll play with leaves and flowers but Harford convinces me that stems and roots are also used in cooking and he gives us a recipe for Yarrow Purée. Thank you, Robin.

It's mid-July and I head out along the country roads that surround me in search of wild yarrow for testing some recipes. I'm not disappointed. I spot a few clumps standing tall and straight, keeping guard over the whimsical faces of Queen Anne's Lace, which nod and wave to me in the light summer breeze. I give blessing to the plants, ask permission, and snip just one flowering stem from a few clumps and the recipes that follow are the result of many pleasant hours spent in the kitchen with yarrow. All recipes ©Pat Crocker.

Harvested and dried yarrow leaves and flowers, garlic scape seed pods, and oregano. *Pat Crocker*

Summer Yarrow Herb Paste

This summer seasoning is fresh and offers a spike of healing sunshine and phytonutrients. I gather a handful of fresh mid-summer herbs and make a small amount of this potent mixture for flavouring potato salad, pasta dishes, sandwich spreads, and soups. The garlic scape seeds (you can substitute fresh garlic) make a moist paste that must be covered and refrigerated. Use it generously because it only keeps for about a week. Salt is optional, but I add half a teaspoon, especially if I'm using the paste to add flavour and balance the blandness of pasta or potatoes.

Makes about 1/2 cup

3 tablespoons chopped fresh oregano or thyme, lemon balm, or sage
Seeds from 6 garlic scape seedpods or 2 fresh cloves garlic
2 tablespoons chopped fresh yarrow flowers and/or leaves
1/4 to 1/2 teaspoon salt

Combine the ingredients in a mortar (or electric spice grinder) and pound using a pestle (or grind) until the mixture forms a rough paste. Transfer to a small jar, cover, and refrigerate for up to 7 days.

Yarrow Syrup

The flavour of yarrow is definitely an acquired taste, which is why I combine it with lighter, sweeter herbs such as lemon balm or sweet cicely. Try using 1/4 to 1/2 cup of this syrup in puddings (see Yarrow Pudding below) or other baked goods. If you plan to use this syrup as a bitter for drinks, experiment with using more yarrow or using yarrow on its own in this recipe. You can add a tablespoon of this syrup to a homemade cough recipe or stir into lemon-ginger tea to help soothe a sore throat.

Makes 1 cup

1 cup water
1 cup sugar
4 sprigs (5 to 7 inches) fresh lemon balm or sweet cicely
2 fresh small yarrow flowers or 1 large fresh flower, coarsely chopped

Ingredients for Yarrow Herb Paste. *Pat Crocker*

Bring the water to a boil over high heat in a heavy, deep saucepan. Lower the heat to medium and stir sugar into the water, whisking until the sugar dissolves. Add herbs and simmer for one minute. Remove from heat, cover, and set aside to steep for 30 minutes, longer for more flavour.

Pour through a mesh strainer into a clean bottle. Cap, label, and store in the refrigerator for up to two months.

Summary Yarrow Soup

Here is where the Summer Yarrow Herb Paste shines! I use a couple of tablespoons, but you can use one tablespoon in step one and another after tasting the soup at the end of cooking. You can also add a cup or two of cooked chicken cubes with the peas in step 2 for a heartier soup.

Makes 6 cups

2 tablespoons olive oil
1 large onion, chopped
2 tablespoons Summer Yarrow Paste
6 cups vegetable or chicken broth, divided
1 cup dried macaroni or orecchiette pasta
2 cups fresh or drained canned corn kernels
1 cup 1-inch cut fresh yellow or green beans
1 cup fresh peas

Heat oil in a large stockpot. Add onion and cook, stirring frequently for 5 minutes. Add paste and 1/2 cup of stock and cook, stirring frequently, until onion is soft. Add 2 1/2 cups stock and bring to a boil. Lower heat and stir in pasta. Simmer, stirring occasionally, for 11 to 15 minutes or until pasta is al dente (not soft).

Add remaining stock, corn, and beans. Bring to a boil, lower heat, and simmer for 4 minutes. Stir in peas (and cooked chicken if using) and simmer for 2 minutes.

Yarrow Fritters

Light and fluffy, these fritters are subtly flavoured by yarrow. For more of a yarrow experience, serve with Yarrow Syrup.

Makes about 6 medium fritters

1/4 cup all-purpose flour
2 tablespoons finely ground yarrow leaves and flowers
1/4 teaspoon grated nutmeg
1/4 teaspoon salt
1 cup 10% cream (half and half)
4 large eggs
2 tablespoons unsalted butter

Combine flour, yarrow, nutmeg, and salt together in a large bowl.

Whisk cream and eggs together in a separate bowl. Whisk for 3 to 5 minutes. Pour over flour mixture and stir just until combined.

Heat butter over medium heat in a large, heavy skillet. For each fritter, ladle 2 ounces of batter into the pan. Cook until the edges are golden brown, flip and cook the other side. Repeat until all of the batter is used.

Serve immediately, hot from the skillet. Drizzle with yarrow syrup or maple syrup if desired.

Yarrow Pudding "Cake" with fresh fruit topping. *Pat Crocker*

Yarrow Pudding

Although not so eggy (or heavy) and with more lemon, my recipe was actually inspired by the following recipe from <u>Mackenzie's 5,000 Receipts,</u> 1829. This is actually a "pudding cake," saucy on the bottom, and cakey on the top. Called "pudding" in Canada and Britain.

For a totally gluten-free version, omit the breadcrumbs and use 2/3 cup ground almonds. If you grind your own almonds, the texture will be slightly rougher than if you use almond meal, which you can purchase from a supermarket.

TANSY PUDDING: "Blanch and pound a quarter of a pound of Jordan almonds; put them into a stew pan, add a gill of the syrup of roses, the crumb of a French roll, some grated nutmeg, half a glass of brandy, two tablespoonsful of tansy juice, 3 oz. of fresh butter, and some slices of citron. Pour over it a pint and half of boiling cream or milk, sweeten, and when cold, mix it; add the juice of a lemon, and 8 eggs, beaten. It may be either boiled or baked."

Makes 6 servings

3 large eggs, separated
1 cup milk
2 teaspoons lemon zest
Juice of 2 lemons (6 tablespoons fresh juice)
2 tablespoons unsalted butter, melted
1/2 cup finely ground blanched almonds or almond meal
2 tablespoons dried breadcrumbs
1/4 teaspoon salt
3/4 cup granulated sugar
1/4 cup Yarrow Syrup or maple syrup

Preheat oven to 350°F and lightly grease a 2-quart ovenproof dish.

Whisk egg yolks, milk, lemon zest, lemon juice, and butter together in a large bowl. Add the almonds, breadcrumbs, salt, sugar, and syrup and stir until smooth.

Beat egg whites in a separate, deep bowl using electric beaters. Beat until soft peaks form. Spoon half of the egg whites into the egg yolk mixture and gently fold mixture over the whites until incorporated. Repeat with the remaining egg whites.

Pour the batter into the baking dish and set it into a 9- x 13-inch baking pan. Pour warm water into the baking pan until it reaches halfway up the baking dish. Transfer baking dish in the pan of water to the preheated oven. Bake for 50 to 60 minutes or until the cake is puffy and lightly golden on top. Remove baking dish from the water bath and set aside to cool for about 15 minutes.

Yarrow Juice

You can add up to 1/4 cup fresh yarrow juice to healing teas, smoothies, and soups. Following is an easy way to juice fresh herbs.

Process 2 or 3 handfuls of fresh yarrow flowers, leaves, and stalks in a food processor until very finely chopped. Place in a square of cheesecloth and squeeze out the juice. Keep in a covered container in the refrigerator for up to 3 days.

Yarrow Cold, Cough, Catarrh & Fever Tea

I have to admit that yarrow hasn't been the first herb I might turn to when a cold threatens. But it is antibiotic and antioxidant and it is also a soothing tonic for the lungs and throat when an angry cough erupts. From my own recent experience, I can attest that not only will yarrow help break up mucous in the lung lining, it also assists in keeping the lungs clear.

To break a fever, pour 1/2 cup boiled water into a cup over 1 tablespoon fresh (1 teaspoon dried) yarrow flowering tops, sweeten to taste with honey. Make this tea and sip hot three or four times per day.

To make 1 cup tea for colds, catarrh, and cough, use yarrow on its own or combine it with one or two other cold- and cough-soothing herbs from the list below.

yarrow (*A. millefolium* or *A. ptarmica*) flower, leaves, or stems

elecampane (*Inula helenium*) chopped fresh or dried root
coltsfoot (*Tussilago farfara*), leaves and flowers
horehound (*Marribium vulgare*) leaves and flowers
mullein (*Verbascum thapsus*) leaves and flowers
peppermint (*Mentha* x*piperita*) leaves and flowers

Measure 1 tablespoon of yarrow and one or two of the herbs listed (or 1 teaspoon each, dried) into a teapot. Pour 1 cup boiled water over and cover the pot. Set aside to steep for at least 10 minutes. Strain into a cup and sweeten to taste with honey. Drink the tea hot or warm and take it three times per day or as often as needed.

Cough Spirit

I wanted to find a way to deliver the antibiotic, cough suppressant, and tonic qualities of some powerful cough, cold and flu herbs without making a traditional syrup using sugar. So when I discovered the following recipe for 'Soup Herb Spirit', I knew that a 'spirit' of cough herbs was just the thing— easy to make, potent, and very easy to take. You can strain and discard the herbs after steeping them in the brandy and even add a tablespoon of liquid honey, but I like to leave the herbs in the jar and simply shake the jar before taking the dose of spirit.

Nowadays, we don't use herbed 'spirits' to flavour food but steeping your favourite dried herbs in brandy would be an interesting, not to mention simple way to spark dressings, sauces, gravy, soup, or stew.

SOUP HERB SPIRIT: "Those who like a variety of herbs in soup, will find it very convenient to have the following mixture. Take when in their prime, thyme, sweet marjoram, sweet basil, and summer savory. When thoroughly dried, pound and sift them. Steep them in brandy for a fortnight, the spirit will then be fit for use."   –*Kitchen Directory*, 1846

White yarrow growing in the garden at Southbrook Winery, Niagara, Ontario.
Pat Crocker

Pat's Cough Spirit

Makes 1 cup

3 tablespoons crushed dried yarrow flower and/or leaves
2 tablespoons crushed dried coltsfoot or hyssop leaves
2 tablespoons crushed dried horehound leaves
2 tablespoons crushed dried mullein leaves
1 cup brandy

Powder the herbs using an electric spice grinder. Transfer to a small jar with a lid. Pour brandy over the herbs, cap and shake well. Label the jar and set in a sunny window for two weeks before using. Store in the refrigerator indefinitely. Take 1 tablespoon as required.

Yarrow Digestive Tea

The bitter quality of yarrow stimulates the digestive system so take this tea about 20 minutes before meals. You can use yarrow alone or combine it with one or two other digestive herbs from the list below.

Makes 1 cup, enough for 3x per day

yarrow (*A. millefolium* or *A. ptarmica*) flowers, leaves or stems
dandelion (*Taraxacum officinale*) leaves or roots
fennel (*Foeniculum vulgare*) seeds
ginger (*Zingiber officinale*) roots
marshmallow (*Althaea officinalis*) roots
peppermint (*Mentha* x*piperita*) leaves and flowers

Measure 1 tablespoon of chopped fresh yarrow plus 1 tablespoon each of two other chopped fresh herbs (or 1 teaspoon each dried herb) into a teapot.

Stir in 1/2 cup boiled water and cover the pot. Set aside to steep for at least 5 minutes.

Add 1/2 cup apple cider vinegar to the pot, stir well, and strain into a clean jar. Store in the refrigerator.

Drink 1/3 cup of the digestive tea about 20 minutes before meals. For best digestive results, do not sweeten the tea.

Yarrow Spring Tonic

Yarrow has been used for centuries as a blood cleanser and for its tonic effect on the lungs. Parsley is a tonic herb. Burdock root is tonic and herbalists use it as a skin, blood, and lymphatic cleanser, soothing demulcent, and to soothe the kidneys. Use all three herbs together with fresh maple sap or syrup for a restorative spring elixir.

Makes 2 servings

Measure 1 tablespoon each, chopped fresh yarrow roots, parsley leaves, and burdock roots (or 1 teaspoon each, dried) into a teapot. Stir in 1 cup boiled water and cover the pot. Set aside to steep for at least 10 minutes.

Taste and add maple sap or maple syrup as desired. Stir well and strain into a clean jar. Store in the refrigerator for up to 2 days.

Drink 1/2 cup of the tonic first thing in the morning for a few days around Spring Equinox.

Footnotes
[1.] Dalecarlian- A group of Scandinavian people living in Dalarna County, Sweden.

References

Harford, Robin. "Eatweeds." https://www.eatweeds.co.uk/yarrow-achillea-millefolium#:~:text=Spring%20to%20Autumn.-,Food%20Uses%20of%20Yarrow,butter%20as%20a%20side%20dish. Accessed 7-10-23.

Hutchens, Alma R. *Indian Herbalogy of North America.* Shambhala, 1991. p. 313.

Le Strange, Richard. *A History of Herbal Plants.* Arco Publishing Company Inc., 1977.

Loewenfeld, Claire and Philippa Back. *The Complete Book of Herbs and Spices.* Little, Brown and Company, 1974.

Meyer, Joseph E. *The Herbalist*. MeyerBooks, 1918, 1932, 1960, 1986.

Sumner, Judith. *The Natural History of Medicinal Plants*. Timber Press, Inc., 2000.

Pat Crocker's mission in life is to write with insight and experience, cook with playful abandon, and eat herbs with gusto. She is happiest when sharing what she knows about whole foods and eating to be healthy.

As a professional Home Economist (BAA, Toronto Metropolitan University) and Culinary Herbalist, Pat's passion for healthy food is fused with her knowledge and love of herbs. She has honed her wellness practice over more than five decades of growing, photographing, and writing about what she calls *the helping plants*. In fact, Crocker infuses the medicinal benefits of herbs in every original recipe she develops.

An award-winning author—she received the Herb Society of America Award for Excellence in Herbal Literature—Pat has written 23 herb/healthy cookbooks, including *The Herbalist's Kitchen*, *The Healing Herbs Cookbook*, and *The Juicing Bible*.

Yellow-blooming yarrow, *Achillea filipendulina*, has naturalized worldwide and is second to the white-blooming in medicinal properties. *Susan Belsinger*

Really Bitter Yarrow Bitters in the making. *Karen England*

Yarrow Through the Seasonings

Karen England

Yarrow, *Achillea millefolium*, is a wholly bitter herb but, albeit counter-intuitive, the bitterness is commonly referred to as "pleasant" or "sweet" by those who eat and drink fresh and dried yarrow. When used judiciously in various seasoning blends, it adds a lovely bitter umami aspect to them, especially in bitters, which have been referred to as the seasoning blends of cocktails, as well as salts, peppers, sugars and spice blends.

The Seasonings

The following recipes are for yarrow-forward seasoning blends as well as some recipes and ideas for using them.

My bitters recipes are all one step, and super easy, but if you wish to make even better bitters that are still easy but with more than one step, see Susan Belsinger's wonderful chapter "all about bitters" in her book *the perfect bite*.

Really Bitter Bitters – aka Yarrow Bitters

Yarrow is so bitter an herb that it was a no brainer to use it to make bitters. I sometimes use two kinds of homemade bitters in a cocktail recipe, so I am also including the Lemon Bitters recipe for this reason. Note: commercial bitters are usually made with 70- to 90-proof alcohol, so using common, easily obtainable 80-proof liquor in the making of homemade bitters is fine even if the recipe calls for higher proof.

4 ounces fresh or 2 ounces dried yarrow flowers and leaves
2 ounces whole allspice berries
1 ounce whole coriander seeds
8 ounces (possibly more) Everclear (121 proof), overproof or 100-proof vodka, or cask-strength whiskey

Put the yarrow, allspice and coriander into a sterilized quart mason jar with a lid. Pour the alcohol over to cover the herbs and spices completely. Seal with a lid and set aside at room temperature for a month. Shake gently to agitate every few days.

After a month, strain into a clean bottle or jar, label and date. Use in the following recipes or any recipe calling for bitters.

Lemon Bitters

1 large wax-free lemon, washed and zested with a vegetable peeler, pulp reserved
1 ounce allspice berries (about 2 tablespoons), slightly crushed with a mortar and pestle
1/2 ounce cinnamon sticks, about 1 tablespoon crushed with a mortar and pestle
2 to 3 fresh or dried bay leaves, broken or crumbled fine
8 ounces (possibly more) 100-proof vodka

In a sterilized quart mason jar with a lid put the lemon zest and pulp, allspice, cinnamon, and bay. Pour the alcohol over to cover the fruit and spices completely. Seal with a lid and set aside at room temperature for a month. Shake gently to agitate every few days.

After a month, strain into a clean bottle or jar and use in the following recipes or any recipe calling for bitters.

Seasoned Salt with Yarrow

Use in any recipes calling for seasoned salt.

Yield: about 1/3 cup

3 heaping tablespoons Maldon or other sea salt
1/2 tablespoon ground celery seeds
1/2 tablespoon sweet paprika
1/2 tablespoon dried yarrow leaves
1 teaspoon granulated garlic
1/2 teaspoon sugar
1/2 teaspoon granulated onion
1/4 teaspoon cayenne
1/4 teaspoon turmeric powder
Finely grated zest of one lemon (Don't worry, all the salt and other dried spices in this recipe will quickly desiccate the fresh lemon zest.)

Combine all the above ingredients in a clean glass jar with a tight-fitting lid.

Dried yarrow leaves ground to a powder in a mortar. *Karen England*

Tomato Water Martinis. The glasses are rimmed with delicious Yarrow Seasoned Salt and the cocktails are garnished with tiny tomatoes threaded onto fresh yarrow stems. *Karen England*

Trader Moe's Flower Pepper with Yarrow

Many years ago my dearest friend, Maureen, aka Moe, contacted me very upset because the chain of Trader Joe's grocery stores discontinued her favorite seasoning blend of theirs called "Flower Pepper" and she wondered if I could recreate it for her. I'd never heard of it but told her I would see what I could do and this recipe is the result. I make this for her every year for Christmas—it makes a great gift!

Makes approximately 1 cup

1/3 cup rainbow peppercorns
1/8 cup each of the following dried flowers: calendula blossoms, cornflower petals, lavender florets, red rose petals and yarrow flowers

Leave all of the ingredients whole and store in a glass jar with a tight-fitting lid and grind only as needed to maintain freshness.

For best results in recipes, grind first before measuring. Use in recipes calling for seasoned pepper.

The Drinks

Tomato Water Martini

Inspired by the Black Martini recipe in the book <u>Tomatomania!</u> by Scott Daigre. According to Tomatomania! about Tomato Water: "All that great clear juice inside the tomato cavity has a subtle but distinct tomato flavor, very different from store-bought juice. Use tomato water to poach seafood and chicken, blanch vegetables, or as a cocktail base. To save tomato water: As you chop tomatoes, dump any juice that accumulates on your board directly into a bowl, easy as that."

Makes one drink

Yarrow Seasoned Salt
1 ounce gin, such as Aviation
1 ounce vodka, such as Titos

Cucumber Water Martinis are a simple variation on the Tomato Water Martini.
Karen England

1 ounce tomato water, see recipe introduction
6 to 8 drops/dashes Yarrow Bitters

Sprinkle some Yarrow Seasoned Salt onto a plate that is wider than a martini glass. Using water, barely moisten the rim of the glass and dip the damp rim into the yarrow salt. Put the seasoned-salt-rimmed glass into the freezer or refrigerator to chill.

In a cocktail shaker add the gin, vodka and tomato water. Add lots of ice and shake or stir until well chilled.

Strain into the chilled, salt-rimmed glass. For the garnish, use several tiny or a couple of cherry tomatoes threaded onto the stem of fresh or dried yarrow.

Cucumber Water Martini Variation

Makes one drink

Following the previous recipe, substitute cucumber water for the tomato water, by chopping a cucumber and draining the solids in a colander over a bowl to obtain just the liquid.

Instead of threading tiny tomatoes on a yarrow stem for garnish, I use a cucumber peel ribbon wrapped fetchingly around the yarrow stem instead.

Garnishing options for Manhattans and other cocktails. Thread dried cherries onto the stems of herbs or edible flowers such as yarrow, rosemary, bay, scented pelargonium, lavender and rose hips. Using a string of lemon zest, try tying a cute lemon peel bow onto the stems of cocktail cherries.
Karen England

Even More Perfect, Perfect Manhattans being yarrow smoked. *Karen England*

Even More Perfect, Perfect Manhattan Cocktail

I learned, while sitting at a bar in Manhattan, New York, just what a "perfect" Manhattan cocktail was, and it was the "perfect" place to learn such a thing! The drink was not quite what I had assumed when ordering. The good folks at Liquor.com explain the Perfect Manhattan better than I can thusly ...

"Many drinkers will agree that the standard Manhattan is a perfect cocktail: simple, balanced and elegant. But the Perfect Manhattan is in fact a separate, though closely related, drink; the 'Perfect' in the drink's name refers not to a cocktail made perfectly (though that is, of course, the aim) but rather to the use of two different styles of vermouth in 'perfect'—which is to say, equal—proportions."

Well, for me, that is indeed a wonderful drink, but I have taken the perfect concept and run with it, increasing the perfection (if such a thing is possible) with my version which uses equal proportions of everything, not just the vermouth. Of course, you can feel free to dial back the perfection a tad and use only one type of cherry garnish.

Makes one drink

1 ounce bourbon whiskey, such as Bulleit
1 ounce rye whiskey, such as Rittenhouse
1/2 ounce sweet vermouth, such as Dolin
1/2 ounce dry vermouth, such as Martini & Rossi
5 to 6 drops/dashes Yarrow Bitters
5 to 6 drops/dashes Lemon Bitters
Several dried cherries threaded onto a yarrow, rosemary or other herbal stem, and several maraschino-style stemmed cherries, for double the garnish

Karen's How-to-Smoke a Cocktail

Optionally for fun, the aforementioned cocktail, complete with its garnishing, gets an added treatment of being yarrow "smoked" (remember I said optional) before serving. Why yarrow smoked, you ask? Well, you may not have noticed but smoked cocktails are all the rage in bars these days. I've enjoyed everything from a rosemary-smoked scotch to an oakmoss-smoked old-fashioned cocktail in the last few months and decided to give a yarrow-

smoked drink a try at home. Not wanting to spend any money on cocktail smoking equipment (which can be quite pricey) I hacked the setup detailed below to successfully smoke drinks, not just the Even More Perfect, Perfect Manhattans, using items already in my kitchen and probably also in yours.

Gather the smoking supplies listed below:
2-gallon size Anchor Hocking (or similar) glass jar
2 large wooden spoons
2 small glass bowls
2 freshly made cocktails in stemmed glasses
Dried yarrow flowers, or other herbs such as lavender, rosemary, bay, etc. for smoking
Matches or lighter

Make the cocktails, pour them into the stemmed glasses and garnish the drinks.

Put a small handful of dried yarrow blossoms or herbs or other flowers of your choosing in the two little bowls and light them on fire—my yarrow really only smoldered.

Once smoldering, place the cocktails and the yarrow bowls closely together on a counter or cutting board and lay the two spoons along the outside; this is so there is some airflow in the jug.

Upend the glass jar over the drinks and smoking flowers, resting the opening of the jar on the spoons.

Leave for several minutes for the smoke to permeate the jug and the drinks.

Remove the jar, put out the fire and serve the smoked drinks!

Karen's Basic Manhattan Cocktail

Not interested in all this perfection? Use the Really Bitter Yarrow Bitters to make a great unsmoked, classic Manhattan cocktail.

Makes one drink

2 ounces Rye or Bourbon whiskey

1 ounce sweet vermouth
5 to 6 drops/dashes Yarrow Bitters

Stir with lots of ice in cocktail shaker or pitcher until well chilled.

Strain into a chilled cocktail glass, garnish with a cherry or zest of lemon and serve.

The Nibbles

In my estimation, cocktails always need not only garnishes but nibbles served alongside. Here are some of my favorites utilizing the same yarrow bitters and seasonings as the cocktails.

Deviled Eggs and/or Egg Salad

I make deviled eggs flavored the same as egg salad; but for a lovely uplift to a favorite standard dish, you can add a few dashes of yarrow bitters, if you like, and season liberally with yarrow flower pepper, instead of your usual seasonings.

(My in-the-shell egg cooking method is to steam the eggs in a vegetable steamer for 15 minutes and then immediately plunge the hot eggs into an ice bath to stop the cooking. Cool the eggs completely before peeling. Note: I have egg-laying hens and have learned that very fresh eggs from the coop are impossible to peel when hard cooked. Use older eggs for the best results.)

Makes 8 deviled eggs or enough egg salad for 2 sandwiches

4 large hard-cooked eggs
1/4 cup mayonnaise
2 to 3 tablespoons cream, milk or water
1 tablespoon olive oil, optional
1 tablespoon finely chopped flat-leaved parsley, plus more leaves for garnish
1/2 tablespoon freshly ground Trader Moe's Flower Pepper
1 to 2 teaspoons prepared mustard, to taste
1/4 teaspoon sea salt
Few dashes Tabasco sauce
Pinch of paprika, plus more for dusting the finished eggs

For the deviled eggs, halve the eggs and separate the yolks into a bowl.

For the egg salad, chop both the egg whites and yolks into a bowl.

Stir the remaining ingredients into either bowl.

For the deviled eggs, spoon the yolk mixture equally into the egg white halves; top each with a dusting of paprika, and a parsley leaf and serve.

Use the egg salad to make sandwiches or stuff large tomatoes.

Kabobs

When using long, fresh or dried yarrow stems as skewers the sky is the limit for what you can thread onto the stems.

Soak the dried yarrow flower heads that are atop the stems for a few minutes in water before grilling to slow the dried skewers from burning while cooking.

I use vegetables such as various colored bell peppers, zucchinis, onion sections, and radishes and grill them, plain (undressed, as the yarrow sticks tend to catch fire.)

Serve them at room temperature dressed with a little olive oil and a sprinkling of Yarrow Seasoned Salt for a delicious nibble.

Try grilling things like shrimp, halloumi cheese and cubed bread separately on yarrow skewers to have more nibble options for everyone.

For an uncooked nibble, consider making a caprese salad on a yarrow skewer with fresh cherry tomatoes threaded along with folded fresh sweet basil leaves and mozzarella pearls. Dress with olive oil and balsamic vinegar seasoned with Trader Moe's Flower Pepper right before serving.

References

Belsinger, Susan. *the perfect bite.* Balboa Press, 2022. pp. 321-33.

Daigre, S., and Garbee, J. *Tomatomania!* St. Martin's Griffin, 2015. pp.140, 145.

Maier, Kathryn. "Perfect Manhattan." *Liquor.com.* www.liquor.com/perfect-manhattan-cocktail-recipe-5094817. Accessed 30 August 2023.

Karen England lives, works and gardens on two steeply sloping acres in Vista, a small town in northern San Diego County, California, just nine miles as a crow flies from the Pacific Ocean. When she's not drinking herbal cocktails, she drinks tea. Find her on Instagram @edgehillherbfarm.

I hope that you will lean-in to the pleasant bitterness that is the herb yarrow, and make these yarrow-forward seasonings, the bitters, flower pepper and seasoned salt and use them often in your foods, drinks and as gifts. *Karen England*

Medicinal Uses of Yarrow

Composi

Achillea Millefolium L.

WMüller n d

Achillea millefolium L. Kohler's Medicinal Plants, Vol. 1, 1887.
Public Domain, *plant illustrations.org*

The Essence of Yarrow

Kathleen Connole

My introduction to the study of the essential oil of yarrow, *Achillea millefolium*, inspired many questions and resulted in a dive into what makes this oil so incredibly powerful, and expensive.

My love of history led to research into the ancient practice of distillation of plants. I discovered that it is likely that the first distillations of the aromatic compounds were intended to produce distilled waters (in particular, rose water), or hydrosols, and that the essential oils floating on the top of the distillate may have at first been discarded. Then, when it was discovered how valuable the essential oils were, the leftover water was considered a mere byproduct.

The earliest distillation of essential oils was practiced in Egypt, Persia, and India, 5000 years ago. One of the most ancient techniques used by Egyptians involved boiling the plant material in large pots covered with shorn fleece or other heavy cloth. The wool acted as a type of condenser, absorbing the aromatic steam. As it cooled and condensed, the fleece was wrung out to extract the aromatic substances and collected in clay vessels (Catty, 2001).

In the Middle Ages a crude form of distillation was used to produce floral waters. In the 17th and 18th centuries the study and use of the essential oils obtained from plants was primarily the focus of apothecaries and pharmacists, and by the 19th century they were widely used in medicine. Gradually they became important to the perfume industry and began to be used as flavorings in foods and beverages. When modern chemistry was able to isolate and synthesize essential oil constituents, the demand for true essential oils decreased in favor of the less expensive synthetics.

The earliest recorded use of *Achillea* essential oil dates to the 1700s. By the 1800s it had become popular in cosmetics and perfumery, and as a pain reliever and wound healer. Its antispasmodic, anti-inflammatory, and antibacterial properties were first tested in medical science to treat breathing, reproductive, and digestive disorders (www.essentially.com).

The first distillation of "a blue volatile oil" from *Achillea* was in 1719. This was the very beginning of yarrow's chemical analysis; by 1916 only two constituents had been identified. Since then, over 120 compounds have been studied.

The blue color, which is due to azulene and related compounds such as chamazulene, has historically been of the greatest interest to chemists. In 1863 the English chemist Septimus Piesse isolated the azure blue chromophore of azulene from yarrow and wormwood. Piesse was instrumental in the development of modern perfumery and invented the concept of "notes" to describe the nature of essential oils as it relates to perfume. These constituents are only available after the steam distillation process (www.en.wikipedia.org/wiki/azulene).

Not all species of *Achillea* possess these compounds. It is interesting to note that current studies reveal that it is absent in *A. millefolium* L. and its subspecies and is found only in the closely related species *A. lanulosa* Nutt. and *A. collina* Becker. *A. lanulosa* is the North American native species, and *A. collina*, commonly known as mountain yarrow, is native to the Mediterranean (www.aromaticstudies.com).The quality of "blue yarrow oil" will also depend upon the time of day that the plant is harvested, the weather during the growing season, and the distillation process that is used. Best practices include gathering the plant material early in the morning when the oil content is the highest, and slow, low-heat distillation to preserve the delicate chemical composition (www.bravenbloom.com).

Chromophore is the term for a molecule which absorbs light at a certain wavelength, emitting color as a result. This was first isolated in the 15th century by the steam distillation of German chamomile. This color is named azulene, after "azul," Spanish for blue. It is found in nature in certain plants including yarrow, chamomile, and tansy, in mushrooms, the oil from a wood called guaiac, and some marine invertebrates. The unusual structure was first reported by a Croation-Swiss chemist, Lavoslav Ružička, in 1937. Ružička went on to win the Nobel Prize in chemistry in 1939; his lifelong work in the chemistry of natural compounds included isolating pyrethrins from *Tanacetum* and the essential oil constituent linalool (www.en.wikipedia.org/wiki/chromophore/ Lavoslav_Ružička).

Today there is a resurgence of interest in the medicinal and aromatic properties of essential oils. They are used in natural perfumery, health and beauty products, and for aromatherapy.

As essential oils have become more popular, their production has become a profitable industry that raises some important ethical questions. Large-scale distillation requires a huge amount of labor. Land use for the monoculture of plant material can result in deforestation, irresponsible agricultural practices, and destruction of the balance of ecosystems.

Some examples of how much plant material it takes to make 16 ounces of an essential oil:10,000 pounds of rose petals, 6,000 pounds of lemon balm; and 250 pounds of lavender flowers (www.rowanandsage.com).

As to why yarrow essential oil is so valuable (and pricey), it takes a metric ton (2,205 pounds) of yarrow plant material to obtain one pint of the essential oil. Mountain Rose Herbs offers certified organic "Blue Yarrow," 5 ml for $31.00; 1/2 ounce for $80.75; and 1 ounce for $124.00. The yarrow essential oil that has a blue color contains the medicinal constituents azulene and the related chamazulene; not all yarrow species possess these chemicals.

As we read the article on yarrow essential oil's many medicinal uses by Dorene Petersen in this book, may we greatly appreciate how powerful this plant's essence truly is. One only needs a few drops of the oil to formulate each of the remedies.

Another issue is that the popularity of essential oils has resulted in such unethical practices as substitutions and adulteration of the pure oils to cut costs and increase profitability. Thus, much care should be taken when purchasing our essential oils; Petersen gives us good advice to consider.

From the article "Sustainable Medicinal and Aromatic Plants: Working towards developing a sustainable value chain of medicinal and aromatic plants through extension of new technologies and practical knowledge among the growers," I learned about a very promising organization called Solidaridad. This group is working with nearly 800 farmers in India, the world's second-largest exporter of medicinal plants. India produces more than 300,000 medicinal preparations that are used in ancient healing systems such as Ayurveda, Unani, and Homeopathy.

The goals of the Solidaridad organization are to improve the quality of herbal products by educating farmers about good agricultural practices, and to create a market for affordable, sustainable, good-quality products. The program has encouraged a shift from cereals and other low-value crops to

Achillea millefolium has white to pinkish blooms; this common yarrow has more medicinal virtues than the colorful cultivars. *Susan Belsinger*

high-value medicinal and aromatic plants. These plants often require less inputs, are more in balance with nature, and increase the farmers' profits at the same time. Yarrow is widely used in Ayurvedic medicine and its ease of cultivation, with few demands upon resources, suggests that it could be a very good choice for this program.

One example of the success of this approach is that farmers who cultivated ashwagandha earned a profit from 0.63 acres equal to that earned from 2.5 acres of wheat. Some other crops being grown in this program, that require less water than wheat, include *Mentha* species, lemongrass, Tulsi, black cumin, and turmeric. Solidaridad is working to implement such sustainable and more environmentally friendly practices in over 40 countries worldwide.

I first learned about hydrosols when, many years ago, Tina Marie Wilcox demonstrated to our Herb Society of America Ozark Unit the home version of the distillation of a hydrosol. I do not remember what herb was used, but the amazing process was done with a large stockpot, a heat-proof container, a brick or flat stone, a heat source, ice, and plant material.

The detailed instructions for making a hydrosol at home can be found at www.nittygrittylife.com, with the recommendation that "All equipment should be impeccably clean."

The year that *Laurus nobilis*, sweet bay, was Herb of the Year, 2009, there was a demonstration of distillation at the Medicinal Herb workshop at the Ozark Folk Center, by some herbal friends from southern Missouri. It took bushels of bay leaves to obtain the tiniest amount of bay essential oil. Our friends mentioned that one of their favorite hydrosols was made from yarrow, which they found to be an effective insect repellent.

The phytochemistry of yarrow is discussed in detail in the articles by Gagnon and Petersen in this book. It is interesting to note that Petersen states that "approximately 21% of the oil dissolves in the distillation water and must be re-distilled and added back into the oil."

The process of redistilling is called cohobation, and since the process recaptures micro drops of essential oils, allowing them to cling together and thus be collected, the yield of essential oil will be greater. However, the hydrosol that results will contain almost no dissolved therapeutic constituents and the repeated heating seems to damage the water-soluble components (Catty, 2001).

Wild yarrow hydrosols, essential oil, and white and pink flower essences.
Kathleen Connole
(background: Wenatchee Foothills, Chelan County, Washington.
www.wikimediacommons)

Hydrosols "hydro," water, and "sol," soluble, are complex mixtures that consist of very diluted solutions of the hydrophilic (water-soluble) constituents of the plant distillate and microscopic essential oils in suspension (generally less than one percent). Although they can be produced as a byproduct of essential oil distillation, the best quality hydrosols are created alone, as important products, rather than as the byproduct. The finest hydrosols are uniform solutions, without any visible oil droplets and are therapeutically more powerful than the complete water collected at the end of essential oil distillation (www.researchgate.net). Other names used include distillates, hydrolates, hydrolats, herbal and aromatic waters, and floral waters, although not all hydrosols are obtained from flowers.

The process of distillation seems magical, as it "brings forth the essence of the plant ... heat, evaporation, transpiration, condensation ... molecules previously held in and between the cell of its parts, reveal themselves to us in an alchemical conglomerate—a hydrosol" (www.aromaticstudies.com).

While the hydrosols that are secondary to essential oil production do possess therapeutic properties and offering them as a product for sale can offset the expense of distilling essential oils, there is a growing awareness that hydrosols are underappreciated and underused. There are advocates who believe that hydrosols should be produced separately, as the intended result, rather than as the byproduct.

According to Jeanne Rose, "... hydrosols should be skillfully produced with artistic precision as the most important products rather than those as side products of distillation; [the water] collected during the early and latter parts of distillation differ in odor notes and chemical composition, as they contain low and high boiling terpenoids, respectively. Hydrosols collected in this manner [are] therapeutically more powerful than the entire distillation water collected at the end of distillation" (Rose, 1999).

Artisanal distillation of hydrosols is described by Jade Shutes as "a ritual undertaking, as the harvesting of healthy plants, in a gratuitous manner, using water from a wild and clean source ... distillation as an act of ritual brings a deeper connection and a greater joy to the ... process and its final products" (www.aromaticstudies.com).

Hydrosols are perishable and subject to contamination, so they should be collected in sterile containers, immediately sealed, and stored in a cool environment or refrigerated. They have a shelf-life of about one year.

Hydrosols lack the hydrophobic elements of essential oils and thus have different aroma profiles. They possess many similar therapeutic properties, but are gentler, without the possible adverse effects, and can be safely applied on skin or taken orally, once diluted further.

"Aromatic waters" (diluted hydrosols) were used as beverages in ancient Persia and continue to be produced and used today. There are currently over 84 manufacturers of these waters; of these 65 still use traditional equipment to distill the waters. Most of these are in the original homeland of the ancient Persians. Plants used include chamomile, caraway, dill, fennel, ginger, lemon balm, parsley, leek, stinging nettle, valerian, horehound, willow, and yarrow. A study published in 2017 examined these aromatic waters and their therapeutic properties. This was done specifically to examine the chemical composition and these waters' use in folk medicine for women's hormonal and reproductive health conditions. Few such studies have ever been done (www.ncbi.nlm.nih.gov).

Such aromatic waters created from distilling yarrow flowers have been used for centuries for blood cleansing, to treat dysmenorrhea, as a nerve tonic, anti-epileptic, cardiotonic, anti-hemorrhoid, antipyretic, antispasmodic, anti-inflammatory, and as a digestive.

Suzanne Catty, author of *Hydrosols: The Next Aromatherapy*, describes the many redeeming qualities of hydrosols. Since they are water-soluble, they are gentler, and can be diluted down to homeopathic proportions. Catty describes yarrow hydrosol as "beautiful to work with" (Catty, 2001).

In the article "Uses and Applications of Yarrow Hydrosol" Jeanne Rose with Len and Shirley Price list the following: Analgesic, anticoagulant, anti-inflammatory, antiviral, bactericidal, calming, wound-healing, circulatory—lowers blood pressure, decongestant, digestive, expectorant, febrifuge, lipolytic, mucolytic, sedative, stimulating, tonic; and that it is good for acne, damaged skin, cellulite, and for spiritual healing and auric work (www.aromaweb.com).

The aroma of yarrow hydrosol is not floral, and to some not really at all pleasant. I can honestly say that I would agree and will be adding a few drops of a complementary essential oil to the ones that I have obtained.

Another way in which we can benefit from this amazing herb's blooms is with its flower essence, as in the gentlest form that there is, the homeopathic flower remedy. I first learned about the Bach flower remedies when my naturopath physician prescribed them to help deal with the grief of losing our first-born daughter to cancer. Yarrow was not among the flower remedies that she recommended, but Gert Coleman's article in this book suggests that it could certainly help to "relieve the physical and emotional suffering undergone through grief."

Flower essences follow the principles of homeopathy, that the life force and vibrational signature of the plant are imprinted within a water-based matrix through sun-steeping the flowers in water. All plants carry vibrational energy patterns, and "flowers are the pinnacle of this energy … [they] work by the principle of resonance within the subtle human energy field, which impacts one's physical and emotional health" (Jenna Carrol, www.endeavor.edu.au).

Dr. Edward Bach, a well-known physician, bacteriologist, and pathologist, developed 12 flower remedies in the 1920s to 1930s. Each remedy was from a plant whose floral essence was associated with a basic human emotion; the originals were known as "The Twelve Healers." In Bach's words: "Healing on an emotional level has knock-on effects on other levels. A healthy emotional life and a balanced personality will allow your body to find its own natural state of health."

Dr. Bach's "sun method" for the more delicate flowers (I can just imagine how lovely this process would be; in itself restoring and rejuvenating.):

"Choose a sunny, cloud-free morning. Fill a small fine glass bowl with pure spring water. Gently snip the flowers directly onto the water's surface or cover the palm of your hand with a broad leaf so that you can then tip the flowers directly onto the water without touching them.

Stay calm, take your time. Enjoy the experience and remember to take a moment to thank the plant when you have finished" (www.bachcentre.com). The heat of the sun transfers the energy of the flowers to the water. This energized water is then filtered, and an equal quantity of brandy is added. This creates the "mother tincture," which is further diluted, using a ratio of 2 drops to 1 ounce of brandy, to create the remedy.

These instructions were never patented and instead were published in Bach's *The Bach Remedies, Illustrations, and Preparations.* Today several companies make the Bach flower remedies from plants that grow in the Bach Centre's Garden in England, including Nelson's, one of the original three pharmacies, which prepares and distributes remedies from the mother tinctures. There are 38 remedies available, including some from other companies that make their own brands.

According to Jenna Carrol, naturopath with the Endeavor College of Natural Health, flower essence therapy has been used for thousands of years to heal physical and emotional imbalances. "Many healers throughout history understood physical manifestations of disease to be a result of emotional imbalance, and these theories are now being corroborated as science and research advances."

A beautiful story from 12th century Europe describes Abbess Hildegard von Bingen placing muslin sheets over flowers at night to absorb their dew, which she then collected in the morning, wrung out, and used to treat people with emotional imbalances (www.endeavor.edu.au).

The flower essence of pink blooming yarrow is especially recommended for those who are very sensitive to negative thoughts and emotions, who can tend to be over-empathetic with others. The white blooming yarrow can give protection against the stress of "environmental energies," such as regular use of today's electronic technology, and life in the city without access to nature.

The overall positive effects of using flower essences may include greater peace and calmness during stressful times, a more joyful and optimistic outlook, forgiveness towards oneself, and greater clarity and focus with insight into life's purpose and direction.

> *"And may we ever have joy and gratitude in our hearts that the Great Creator of all things, in his love for us, has placed the herbs in the fields for our healing."*

> ---Dr. Edward Bach

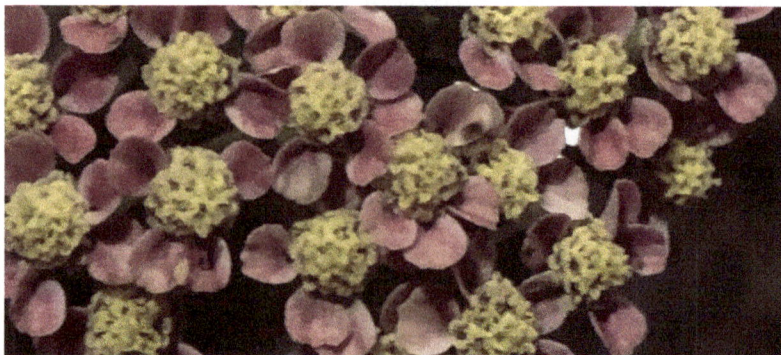

Kathleen Connole bio on page 20

References

"Azulene." www.en.wikipedia.org/wiki/azulene. Accessed 12-3-23.

Carrol, Jenna. "Flower Essence Therapy: What, How, and Why." *Endeavor College of Natural Health.* www.endeavor.edu.au. Accessed 10-26-23.

Catty, Suzanne. *Hydrosols: The Next Aromatherapy.* Healing Arts Press, 2001.

"Chromophore." www.en.wikipedia.org/wiki/chromophore. Accessed 12-3-23.

Devon. "How to Make an Aromatic Hydrosol at Home Without a Still." www.nittygrittylife.com/how-to-make-a-hydrosol/. Accessed 11-10-23.

"The Future of High-Value Medicinal and Aromatic Plants." www.solidaridnetwork.org/story/the-future-of-high-value-medicinal-aromatic-plants/ 6 May 2022. Accessed 11-13-23.

Hamedi, A. et al. "A Survey on Chemical Constituents and Indications of Aromatic Waters Soft Drinks (Hydrosols)Used in Persian Nutrition Culture and Folk Medicine for Neurological Disorders and Mental Health." *Journal of Evidence Based Complimentary Alternative Medicine.* 22 Oct. 2017. www.ncbi.nlm.nih.gov/pma/articles/PMC5871290/. Accessed 10-25-23.

"Hydrosols Versus Essential Oils." www.rowandsage.com/blog/2021/6/9/hydrosols-vs-essential-oils. Accessed 10-25-23.

"Lavoslav Ružička." www.en.wikipedia.org/wiki/ Lavoslav_Ružička. Accessed 12-3-23.

Price, L., and Price, S. *Understanding Hydrolats: The Specific Hydrosols for Aromatherapy: A Guide for Health Professionals.* Churchill Livingstone, 2004.

Rose, Jeanne. *375 Essential Oils and Hydrosols.* North Atlantic Books, 1999.

"The Simplicity of the Bach System." www.bachcentre.com. Accessed 10-26-23.

Shutes, Jade. "The Magic of Hydrosols." *The School for Aromatic Studies.* www.aromaticstudies.com/the-magic-of-hydrosols/. Accessed 10-11-23.

---. "Yarrow Essential Oil: *Achillea millefolium.*" www.aromaticstudies.com/yarrow-essential-oil-achillea-millefolium/. Accessed 11-10-23.

feathery fine leaves
delicate petaled corymbs
long, firm woody stalks

Susan Belsinger

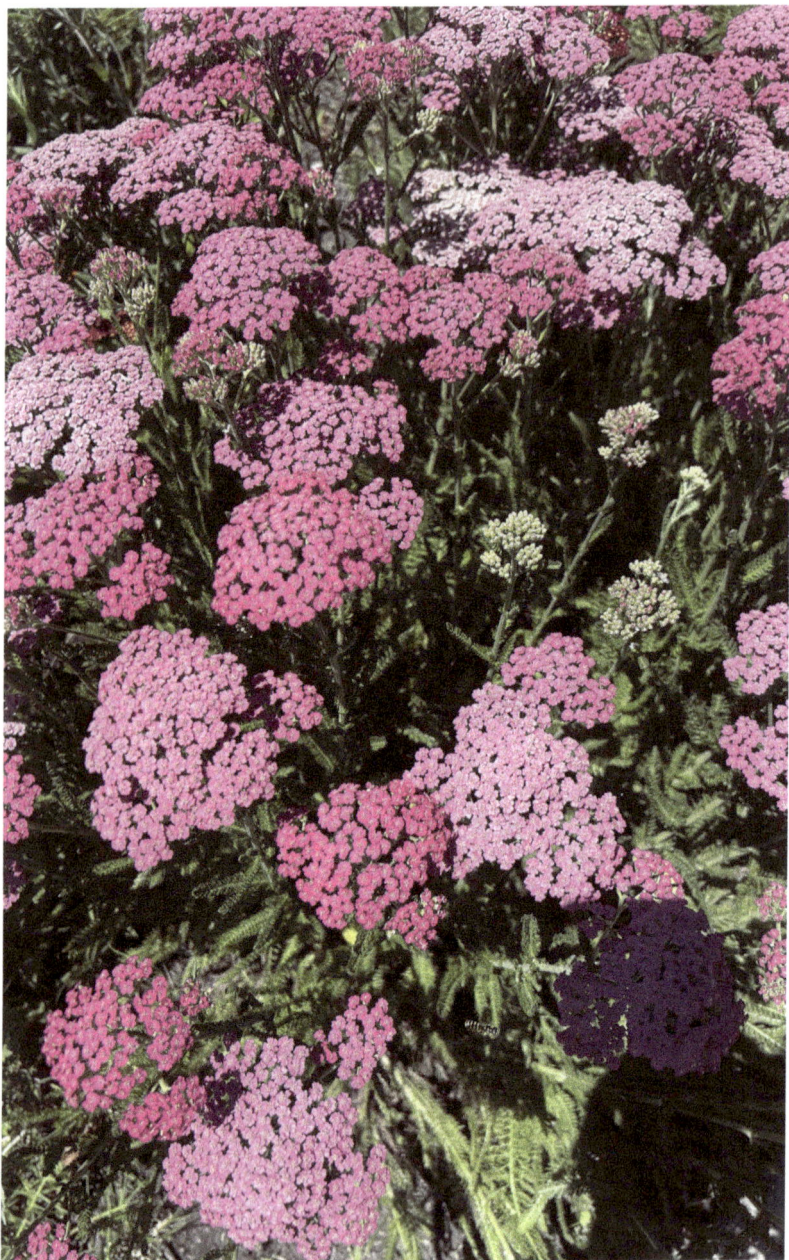

Colorful and bright, pink yarrow cultivars are lovely in the garden and in bouquets. *Janice Cox*

Natural Beauty with Yarrow

Janice Cox

Yarrow is a popular herb plant in many gardens, mine included. I think of it as a "protector plant" for my garden. I have it planted along the entrance to my yard to ward off deer and rabbits that often nibble on my roses and flowers. They do not seem to like the scent and go on down the road, probably to the next house for their evening snack or morning meal. Since I have been planting yarrow, my roses and other flowers have done so much better. I have also read that yarrow may help nearby plants resist disease and improve their fragrance and flavor. It is easy to grow, drought-tolerant and loves the sun. I find that if I have a spot where other plants are not thriving, yarrow usually does well there. Just make sure you have good drainage. It is a wonderful plant for attracting pollinators to your yard. My patch of yarrow seems to attract a variety of insects; even the hummingbirds sometimes take an interest in the red variety. The yellow yarrow is probably the most common one you will see in gardens, but yarrow comes in a variety of colors. I planted a very pretty pink one that is wonderful in cut flower bouquets and for making bath salts. Yarrow is easy to grow and will add beauty to your yard.

Yarrow is also a useful plant in making body care products. It has antibiotic and anti-inflammatory properties, and is cooling, soothing, and healing when used in skin care preparations. It can be added to bath products and used in making soaps, creams, and infusions. I love to cut fresh yarrow in the spring and summer and dry it for year-round use. This also keeps my plants healthy and blooming. Cutting or deadheading your plants will give you a second bloom depending on your growing zone. A strong tea or infusion of yarrow leaves makes a healing skin tonic that can be used to treat insect bites or calm sunburn. You can easily infuse oils, butters, witch hazel, salt, and honey with dried or fresh yarrow flowers and leaves. Note: when infusing oils and butters, you should use only dried plant material, so you do not introduce any extra moisture, which could cause bacteria to grow.

Here are some of my favorite recipes using this beautiful herb:

Yarrow Skin Toner

Yarrow makes a soothing skin astringent or toner that can be used after cleansing to help reduce redness and inflammation. It works well in treating troubled skin, insect bites and calming sunburns.

Makes about 1 cup

1 cup vodka or witch hazel
1/2 cup fresh or 1/4 cup dried yarrow flowers

Place vodka or witch hazel and yarrow in a clean glass jar.

Cover with a tight-fitting lid and place in a cool dark spot.

Let sit for several weeks, gently shaking every now and then; I usually do this every two days.

Strain the liquid and discard the yarrow plant material. Pour into a clean container, label and date.

To use: Apply to your skin using cotton pads or pour into a spray bottle and gently spray onto your skin.

Yarrow Cucumber Cleanser

Cucumber is naturally cleansing and calming to your skin. When you combine it with fresh yarrow flowers you have a mild cleanser that can be used in place of soap for all skin types. This recipe does contain fresh cucumber which has a limited shelf life, so for best results do not double the recipe and store any leftover cleanser in the refrigerator.

Makes about 1/2 cup

1 whole cucumber
1 tablespoon fresh yarrow flowers and leaves or 1/2 tablespoon dried yarrow flowers and leaves
1/2 cup water (non-chlorinated)
1 teaspoon honey

In a blender or food processor combine cucumber, yarrow, water, and honey and process on high until you have a well-blended mixture.

To use: Massage into your skin and let sit for a few seconds up to a minute. Then rinse with warm water followed by a cool water rinse and pat your skin dry.

Yarrow Facial Steam

A facial steam bath is an easy, inexpensive, and therapeutic way to deep cleanse your skin. Gently steaming the skin creates perspiration, which aids in the elimination of toxins, boosts circulation, and softens the skin. Using dried herbs such as yarrow boosts the cleansing effects of the facial steam and helps to soothe and heal your skin. This is a treatment that works well for troubled or oily skin types.

Yield: 1 treatment

3 tablespoons fresh or 1 1/2 tablespoons dried yarrow leaves and flowers
6 cups boiling water

Secure your hair and cleanse your face as you would normally.

Place the yarrow in a large ceramic bowl or basin.

Pour the boiling water over the herb and stir.

Keep your face at least 12 inches above the bowl. Lean over bowl. Cover your head with a towel to keep steam in.

Close your eyes and let the herbal steam open your pores. This should take about 8 to 10 minutes.

Rinse your face with warm water and then cool water, and gently pat your skin dry.

Your skin may be sensitive after this treatment so stay indoors for at least an hour to allow your pores to close completely.

Yarrow Lotion

Yarrow is similar to chamomile as a skin soother; it contains over 50 percent azulene, a well-known anti-inflammatory. It was believed to be a "magic" herb by the early Saxons, who settled in England in A.D. 500. They wore amulets of yarrow to protect them from just about everything. I created this lotion to soothe a bad rash on my arms. It worked like a charm and my rash soon disappeared.

Makes about 3/4 cup

1 tablespoon dried yarrow flowers
1 cup boiling water
1/8 teaspoon baking soda
1 tablespoon jojoba oil
1/3 cup sunflower oil
1 teaspoon grated beeswax

Place the yarrow flowers in a heatproof container.

Pour the boiling water over them and allow to sit overnight or for 8 hours.

Strain the flowers out of the water.

Measure 1/2 cup of the yarrow infusion and add the baking soda, stirring until well mixed. Set aside.

(The remainder of the infusion can be saved for another recipe or used on its own as a toner or in the bath.)

Mix together the oils and beeswax in a glass measuring cup or jar and place the container of oil and beeswax in a pan of water (about 1 to 2 inches of water), making a water bath.

Heat over medium heat until the beeswax is melted (8 to 10 minutes), stirring occasionally.

When the wax is melted, bring the yarrow water/baking soda solution almost to boiling, so it is very hot.

Remove the oil-beeswax mixture from the water bath.

Slowly add the yarrow water/baking soda to the oil-beeswax mixture, stirring briskly. (You can also put the mixtures in the blender and process on high.)

Allow the lotion to cool completely.

The consistency may seem a bit thin, but it will thicken as it cools. The lotion will be pale yellow in color.

Pour the lotion into a clean container with a lid, label and date.

To use: massage a small amount into your skin.

Saturn's Aftershave

In Roman mythology, Saturn is the Roman god of agriculture who fled from Mount Olympus and settled in Italy. There he established a golden age in which all people were equal, and harvests were plentiful. Ancient Romans held a seven-day festival, which was named the Saturnalia in honor of this god. This fresh scent full of harvested herbs and spices would have been perfect to wear during this time of unrestrained celebration.

Makes about 1 cup

1 tablespoon fresh or 1/2 tablespoon dried yarrow flowers
1 tablespoon fresh or 1/2 tablespoon dried sage leaves
3 bay leaves
1 teaspoon dried cardamom seeds, crushed or left whole
5 black peppercorns, crushed or left whole
2 whole clove buds, crushed or left whole
1/2 cup vodka (optional; you can also use all witch hazel)
1/2 cup witch hazel
1 teaspoon vegetable glycerin

Place the fresh yarrow, sage, and bay leaves, cardamom, peppercorns, and clove buds into a clean jar or bottle.

Pour the vodka, witch hazel, and glycerin over them; shake gently.

Cover the bottle top and let sit in a cool, dark spot for two weeks.

Stain the liquid and discard any solids.

Pour your cologne into a clean bottle with a tight-fitting lid, label and date.

To use: Apply as you would any aftershave or cologne product.

A few notes on using Yarrow in body care products:

- Know your source. Make sure the yarrow you are using has been grown organically and has not been sprayed with any pesticides or floral preservatives. If you are unsure, it is probably best to not use.
- When using yarrow in recipes you will want to use double the amount of fresh yarrow versus dried yarrow. It is important to only use dried yarrow when infusing oils and butters.
- When harvesting and drying your yarrow flowers and leaves make sure you make small bundles or place on drying racks where they will get plenty of air flow. For best color results store in a dark, dry spot.
- Yarrow makes a relaxing bath. Fill a muslin tea bag with a few flower heads and some leaves and toss in your tub as it fills. Yarrow is healing and soothing and will boost your circulation.
- If you cut yourself shaving or for any minor cut or scrape, use a fresh yarrow leaf applied directly to your skin to help it heal.
- A strong tea made from yarrow leaves works as a healing mouth rinse for sore gums.

Janice Cox is a garden writer and natural beauty expert. She is the author of *Beautiful Flowers, Beautiful Lavender, Beautiful Luffa, Natural Beauty at Home, Natural Beauty from the Garden, Natural Beauty for All Seasons* and the newly released *Natural Beauty at Home Handbook.* She was the beauty editor for *Herb Quarterly* magazine for more than twenty years. She is the education chair for The Herb Society of America and a member of the International Herb Association. She makes her home in southern Oregon.

Common white yarrow, *Achillea millefolium*, has the most medicinal virtues. *Susan Belsinger*

The Medicinal Uses of Yarrow (*Achillea millefolium* et al.) [Asteraceae]

Daniel Gagnon, Medical Herbalist RH (AHG)

Yarrow (*Achillea millefolium* et al.) [Asteraceae] (Zimmerman 2023)

Other Common Names:
Dutch: Duizendblad (Van Hellemont 1986)
English: Yarrow, milfoil, old man's pepper, soldier's woundwort, knight's milfoil, herbe militaris, thousand weed, nose bleed, carpenter's weed, bloodwort, staunchweed, sanguinary devil's nettle, devil's plaything, bad man's plaything, yarroway (Grieve 1971). Noble yarrow, lady's mantle, thousand leaf (Nickell's 1976)
French: Achillée, millefeuille, herbe aux charpentiers, herbe aux coupures, herbe aux militaires, herbe de St. Jean (Valnet 1992)
German: Schafgarbe (gemeine) (Van Hellemont 1986)
Italian: Achillea (Bartram 1998)
Nepalese: Losar (Sen 2020)
Russian: Tysyaschelistnik (one thousand leaves) or Krovavnik (Blood plant, as in stopping blood plant) (Hutchens 1973)
Spanish: Milenrama (Wichtl 2004)

Part Used: The aerial (aboveground) part as well as the root. The flowers have stronger medicinal qualities than the leaves (Foster 1993).

Herbal Properties: Yarrow possesses a multitude of medicinal properties including alterative, analgesic, antibacterial, antihemorrhagic, anti-inflammatory, antimicrobial, antipyretic, antiscorbutic, antiseptic, antispasmodic, antirheumatic, antiviral, aperitif, aromatic, astringent, bitter tonic, carminative, cholagogue, choleretic, diaphoretic, digestive tonic and diuretic (both as a cold tea), emmenagogue, expectorant, hemostatic, hepatic,

It is best to harvest flower heads just as they open before their peak in order to dry them and retain their color. *Susan Belsinger*

hypoglycemic, hypotensive, peripheral vasodilator, relaxant, sedative, spasmolytic, stimulant, styptic (hemostatic), tonic, urinary antiseptic, vermifuge, and vulnerary activities (Bartram 1998, Bone 2003, Duke 2002, Hoffmann 2003, Menzies-Trull 2003, Nickell 1976, Skenderi 2003).

Constituents: Yarrow contains about 0.1 to 1.4% volatile oil composed of azulene (also found in chamomile) as well as α- and ß-pinenes (mostly ß-pinene), caryophyllene, borneol, terpineol, cineole, bornyl acetate, camphor, sabinene, isoartemisia ketone, and sometimes a trace of thujone. Keep in mind that yarrow's constituents and the composition of its volatile oil vary considerably. Pinch some of the flowers between your fingers and smell the aromatics to get an idea of its essential oil content. Like many other herbs, the relative composition of yarrow's constituents varies considerably. This is especially true for its azulene and chamazulene content. In some yarrow subspecies, these constituents may be very high, while in other subspecies, they are virtually absent (Chandler 1982). Other constituents include flavonoids (e.g. rutin, artemetin, apigenin, luteolin, isorhamnetin, quercetin glycoside); tannins; coumarins; sterols (including ß-sitosterol); fatty acids, (linoleic, myristic oleic, palmitic acids and others); sugars (galactose, glucose, sucrose, arabinose, inositol, mannitol and others); alkaloids or bases (like achilleine, betaine, choline, moschatine, trigonelline, betonicine, and stachydrine); phenolic acids (caffeic); amino acids (alanine, glutamic acid, histidine, leucine, lysine, and others); as well as the analgesic salicylic acid have been reported. Over 120 different constituents have been identified so far (Ali 2017, Chandler 1982, Duke 1985, Leung 1996, Wichtl 2004, Wren 1988).

Notes: It is known that thujone is present in yarrow in trace amounts (Leung 1996). In the past, there have been some concerns about using yarrow as a medicinal plant because of its thujone content. These concerns were based on the effect of the alcoholic beverage *absinthe*. Historically, the presence of thujone in absinthe was believed to be dangerous and addictive (Albert-Puleo 1978). It was thought that thujone could cause vertigo, tremors, delirium, mental deterioration, epileptic attacks, hallucination, convulsions, sleeplessness, and insanity (Arnold 1989). Since then, research has shown that the alcohol itself causes all the symptoms described as *absinthism*, including alcohol poisoning and possibly death (Padosch 2006). Recent research on the subject has exonerated thujone (and yarrow) from causing any harm (Lanchenmeier 2006).

Medicinal Uses: Acute states of colds, influenza (flu), Covid-19, and respiratory syncytial virus (RSV) and the fever that often accompany these diseases; loss of appetite; indigestion such as mild colicky pain in gastrointestinal region; chronic diarrhea and dysentery; dyspepsia; gastro-intestinal ulcers; intestinal hemorrhage; bleeding hemorrhoids; uterine hemorrhage; epistaxis (nose bleeds); toothache; profuse protracted (lasting longer than usual) menstruation; lack of menstruation; hypertension; rheumatism; sprains; swollen tissues; rashes; itchy skin; bruises; other skin conditions and wounds. Used as a sitzbath in diseases affecting the pelvic area such as painful spasms (Wren 1988, Foster 1993, Schilcher 1997, Trickey 1998).

Some Introductory Facts About Yarrow

Yarrow is among the most widespread and widely used medicinal plants in the world. It is a native of Eurasia. It is also found throughout North America, and North Africa. I have found it in Northern Ontario, Scotland, Nepal, India, France, Italy, on the island of Mallorca (Spain), and countless other areas and countries.

The genus *Achillea* includes approximately 110 to 140 species worldwide (Ehrendorfer and Guo 2006). When it comes to yarrow (*Achillea millefolium*) there's often an indiscriminate use of the common name yarrow, referring to several different species of *Achillea*. Therefore, when surveying the literature, keep in mind that much of the work reported under "*A. millefolium*" may refer to either *A. millefolium* in the strict sense or it may refer to any of number of other species which have been more recently and narrowly defined (Chandler 1982). In his book *Dictionary of Economic Plants,* Uphof (1968) reports on nine different *Achillea* species (*A. ageratum, A. atrata, A lanulosa, A. millefolium, A. moschata, A. ptarmica, A. santolina,* and *A. sibirica*) that are used in herbal medicine.

Yarrow may be one of the oldest herbal remedies known to be used by mankind. Recently it has been found in the calcified dental plaque of Neanderthals from the caves of El Sidrón in Northern Spain. Tooth scrapings from tens of thousands of years ago suggest that they may have chewed on medicinal plants to self-medicate and take care of health issues. Scientists concluded that the plant material found in the calculus was most likely yarrow (Hardy 2016).

A close relative of yarrow found in China, *Achillea alpina* is named *shi cao* and has been used in Traditional Chinese Medicine (TCM) for literally thousands of years. This yarrow relative is known as alpine yarrow and sometimes referred to as Chinese yarrow or Siberian yarrow. Shi cao (alpine yarrow) is one of 250 herbs listed in the book *Sheng Nung Ben Cao Chien* (*The Herbal Classic of the Divine Plowman*) written around 2,800 years BCE. This book is known as the first Chinese text to record the healing properties of herbs. In it, legendary Emperor Sheng Nung classified alpine yarrow as an "upper class" herb. Another Chinese medicine book titled *Ben Cao Gang Mu*, written in the 16th century, is known as the *Compendium of Materia Medica*. It has been described as the most complete and comprehensive medicinal herb book ever written in the history of TCM. In it, shi cao is described as being "useful in treating abdominal fullness." In China, folk medicine uses of alpine yarrow include the treatment of abdominal pain, menopause, wound infections, internal bleeding, hemorrhoids, ulcers of the digestive tract, and snake bites (Huang 1993).

It has been said that *Achillea* owes its name to mythology. During the Trojan War (1200 BCE) Achilles was struck by a poisoned arrow shot by Paris. On Venus's advice, Achilles made a poultice from this herb to relieve suffering from his wound. Yarrow has the reputation of being a powerful wound healing agent. In herbal medicine, such an herb is called a vulnerary (herb used in the healing of wounds). Prior to antibiotics, many French soldiers knew of this plant as the soldier's herb. It was referred to by infantrymen as "field bandage" and what made it desirable was that it was available almost everywhere (Leclerc 1976).

On this side of the world, the American anthropologist Daniel Moerman (1998) recorded 377 distinct yarrow medicinal use reports by no fewer than 76 Native American ethnic groups. Of all the herbs he recorded, yarrow had the most medicinal use reports of any plant. Moerman reported that the most common uses were skin problems and injuries (79 reported uses), respiratory illnesses and digestive problems, toothaches (14) and eye problems (9). Chandler (1982) asserts that yarrow is used for a very wide range of health issues worldwide, some of them apparently contradictory. For example, in one culture yarrow is used for abnormally heavy bleeding while in another, it is used for the lack of menstruation. Another example of the amphoteric (a normalizing effect) property of yarrow is that the stimulating effect of the constituent thujone as well as the spasmolytic effects of the flavonoids may be responsible for the seemingly contradictory effects of the herb on the uterine muscles. Yarrow can stimulate the uterus and increase uterine muscular tone without creating spasms, or it can act as a uterine relaxant to relieve uterine pain (Trickey 1998). Because of its amphoteric properties, this herb is, without a doubt, a blessing to womankind.

The Medicinal Proprieties of Yarrow

Over 45 years ago, as a young budding herbalist, yarrow was the first plant that revealed to me the power of herbal medicine. Since then, I have experienced first-hand the incredible healing properties of this plant time and time again. Let me share with you some of its most powerful properties.

Yarrow and its fever-breaking properties

To satisfy my needs for healthy foods in a relative food wasteland, I started a natural food store in my hometown. Hearst, a small town of 5,000 people in Northern Ontario, Canada, is where I first honed my skills as an herbalist. In the first month of opening my store, on a late afternoon, a friend came by and asked me what herb his wife should take to break her fever. She had contracted the flu, was in bed with a 102°F fever, and was shivering and hurting all over. I gave him 2 ounces of yarrow tops I had picked during that summer. I suggested he prepare a cup of yarrow tea, draw a hot bath, and have her drink this tea while soaking in the hot bath. I further instructed him that, when she started sweating, to help her back to bed and let her sweat it out. After work, I drove to his house and learned that within a few minutes of being in the hot bath and drinking yarrow tea, she started to sweat profusely. He helped her change her drenched garment twice from the intense sweating. Three hours after the tea and hot bath, her temperature had dropped to 99°F. The next day, she felt much better and a few days later, she returned to work at the local hospital where she worked as a nurse. Today, I produce a tea named *Sweat Tea* that consists of equal parts of yarrow tops, elder flowers, and peppermint leaves. Full disclosure: I did not create this formula, it's an old classic recipe found in my extensive research and reading about herbs. For over 40 years, I have used this formula successfully for early stages of fevers in colds, flu, and other acute viral infections. For years, our customers have sung the praises of this formula. Years later, I learned why it made scientific sense to use this herb for fevers. Yarrow possesses several constituents with activity that are equal or greater than indomethacin, a nonsteroidal anti-inflammatory drug (NSAID) often used to break fevers (Choudhary 2007). David Hoffmann (2003) affirms that yarrow is an important diaphoretic (induces perspiration) herb and is a standard remedy for helping the body deal with fever.

Yarrow and the digestive system

From mouth to large intestine, yarrow offers invaluable support to the whole digestive system.

A water extract of yarrow (a tea made from the flowering tops) has been shown to heal chronic digestive ulcers. That's not surprising considering that the plant contains significant amounts of anti-inflammatory constituents. Among them is azulene, a potent anti-inflammatory substance (Bakun 2021). In a laboratory study, rodents with chronic stomach ulcers were healed by 75% to 90% within seven days with the use of yarrow water extract (a tea). The researchers found these results superior to the pharmaceutical drug ranitidine (known as Zantac®) at a dosage that is easily attainable from the water extract (Cavalcanti 2006). Other anti-inflammatory compounds that have been found in yarrow and are supportive in digestive issues include luteolin and dicaffeoylquinic acids (Villalva 2022).

A related species, *Achillea alexandri-regis*, has been shown to possess similar effects on ulcerated tissues. It exerts significant anti-inflammatory as well as anti-ulcer activities similarly to its relative yarrow (*Achillea millefolium*) (Kundakovic 2000).

Chamomile (*Matricaria chamomilla*) is another well-known plant that is very rich in azulene. It's not surprising that both herbs are often combined and used to treat digestive conditions and ulcers. Both plants can also be used externally to help heal chronic skin ulcers or other skin issues. Don't hesitate to use them together for this purpose.

Used alone, yarrow is an excellent bitter tonic and astringent to boggy, swollen tissues, such as internal ulcerated tissues. French medical doctor and herbalist, Jean Valnet (1992), recommended yarrow for its antispasmodic properties as well as to soothe spasms of the digestive tract and uterine tissues. Another French herbalist, Maurice Mességué (1975), found this herb to be as a superb tonic of the digestive system. He recommended it as a reliable antispasmodic, used it for stomach cramps, and suggested it to expel gas from the intestinal tract. English herbalists and husband and wife team A.W. Priest and L.R. Priest (1983) recommended cold yarrow preparations to stimulate the appetite and tone the digestive system.

Canadian herbalist Alma Hutchens (1973) stated that yarrow was used by Native American tribes as a tonic when suffering from indigestion as well as run-down conditions. She also reported that Russian herbalists recommend yarrow either as an alcohol extract (using, of course, vodka to extract the herbs) or water decoctions for stomach sickness, gastritis, ulcers, dysentery, and diarrhea. It has also been found helpful in looseness of the bowels, intestinal cramps, intestinal pain, loss of appetite, and vomiting. If these claims seem far-fetched, consider the following: Yarrow extract has been studied in the laboratory and showed strong antispasmodic effect when applied to isolated rat intestinal tissue (Yaeesh 2006). Another study demonstrated antispasmodic effects on guinea pig intestinal tissue (Lemmens-Gruber 2006). This last group of researchers showed that flavonoids extracted and concentrated from the herb, including quercetin, luteolin, and apigenin, had potent antispasmodic activities in the same test. They further concluded that the concentration of these flavonoids found in a cup of yarrow tea is sizeable enough to produce significant antispasmodic effects in human beings (Lemmens-Gruber 2006).

Achillea fragrantissima is another relative of yarrow and grows in Egypt. It is traditionally used for its anti-inflammatory and analgesic properties among Sinai inhabitants. Researchers concluded that *Achillea fragrantissima* extracts possess anti-inflammatory, analgesic activities in addition to protective properties in intestinal and gastric tissues. They also reported that the extract from this plant possesses anti-inflammatory and analgesic properties comparable to indomethacin (aka NSAID) and acetyl salicylic acid (aka aspirin). Additionally, they concluded that the extract stopped damage caused by acetic acid to the large intestine in rats (Abdel-Rahman 2015).

Yarrow regulates liver function (Holmes 1989). It has also been used for spleen congestion due to malaria, liver hypertrophy, and biliary insufficiency (Fournier 1948). Yarrow insures good digestive secretory activity in the entire digestive tract (Willard 1992). In a laboratory study, researchers showed that three cups of yarrow tea daily increase the flow of bile considerably (Benedek 2006), thus being an excellent support to healthy digestive function. They concluded that dicaffeoylquinic acids (DCQAs), a compound found in yarrow, was two to threefold more effective than cynarin, the compound thought to give artichoke (*Cinara scolymus*) its considerable choleretic (an herb that stimulates the production of bile by the liver, thereby increasing the flow of bile) action (Benedek 2007).

Yarrow for skin issues

Steven Foster (1993) writes of herb harvesters working at the Shaker herb garden in Sabbathday Lake, Maine who, whenever they cut themselves, would wash the wound, gather yarrow tops, then apply the crushed yarrow as a poultice directly on the wound. He witnessed the bleeding stop rapidly and cuts heal without infections within a few days. He emphasizes the need to clean the cut properly before applying the freshly crushed yarrow poultice. Yarrow is known to speed the healing of slow-healing wounds and reduce skin inflammation (*British Herbal Compendium* 1992). Hutchens (1973)

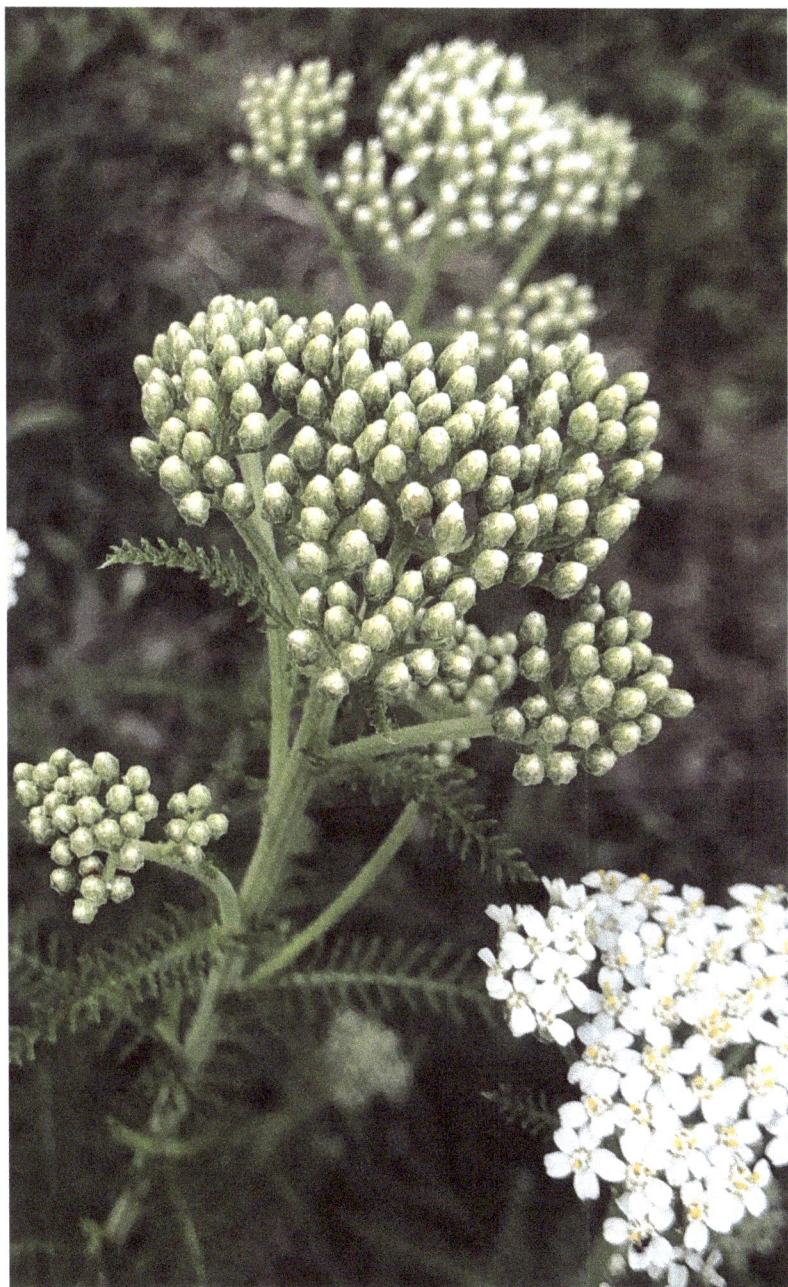

Yarrow buds ready to burst into bloom. *Susan Belsinger*

reported that Native American tribes used the leaves to make a poultice for skin rashes. In Europe, herbalists suggest alcohol extracts of yarrow (and/ or chamomile) to heal skin wounds in children or adults (Bartram 1998). Both yarrow and chamomile have been shown to possess significant anti-inflammatory and bacteriostatic actions. When applying externally to wounds, it's often a good idea to dilute the extract 1:1 or 1:2 with boiled water so it won't sting (Schilcher 1997). Yarrow was shown to be more effective as an anti-inflammatory agent when it is extracted with ethanol (Tadic 2017).

Additionally, acne vulgaris affects 80% of adolescents and at times persists well into adulthood. It can result in scarring and hyperpigmentation. Acne is known to develop in the sebaceous follicles of the cheeks, forehead, chin, and on the back. Recently, researchers have found in yarrow a potent anti-acne constituent named alkamide. They demonstrated that this constituent reduces inflammation, scavenges free radicals, and removes residual pigmentation caused after acne treatment (Shah 2018). It should be used both internally as a tea and externally as a wash.

Yarrow and the circulatory system

Yarrow has a long history of being used for the heart and the circulatory system. Maurice Mességué (1975) used this herb as a heart and circulatory system sedative. He recommended it to individuals who experienced angina and pain in the chest. Since yarrow is rich in flavonoids, including rutin and apigenin, it is an excellent herbal support to tone veins and in varicose veins. It is also used to prevent blood clots and is an effective peripheral vasodilator that opens surface circulatory blood vessels, thus enabling more blood to be circulated freely (Bartram 1998).

Thrombosis occurs when a blood clot forms in an artery or vein. These clots may lead to strokes, heart attacks, peripheral vascular disease, superficial venous thrombosis, deep vein thrombosis (commonly known as DVT) and pulmonary embolism. Each of these types of thrombosis is serious and can be life-threatening. Yarrow is considered a specific remedy for thrombotic conditions associated with hypertension. Apigenin, a flavonoid found in abundance in yarrow, has been found to exert anti-platelet activity, thus preventing blood clot formation (Navarro-Nunez 2008). In England, herbalists often use it to prevent blood clot formation (Bartram 1998). The British Herbal Pharmacopeia (BHP) suggests using yarrow aerial top, stinging nettles (*Urtica dioica*) herb and lime (*Citrus* x*aurantiifolia*) flowers together as a remedy for simple high blood pressure or high blood pressure with thrombosis – either cerebral or coronary (BHP 1983). Yarrow's strong hypotensive, cardiovascular inhibitory and bronchodilatory effects also explain its medicinal use in hyperactive cardiovascular and airway disorders, such as hypertension and asthma (Khan 2010).

Yarrow contains yet another flavonoid named artemetin. An animal study showed that oral administration of artemetin reduced, in a dose-dependent manner, the blood pressure of rats. The results of this study suggest that artemetin may be the main flavonoid responsible for the cardiovascular effects popularly attributed to yarrow. One single dose of artemetin reduced the mean arterial pressure of rats in the range of ~10 mm Hg, even when it was given orally 3 hours before the measurement of blood pressure. That's significant because, in humans afflicted with high blood pressure, it has been estimated that a reduction of 5 mm Hg in mean arterial pressure reduces the mortality due to stroke and coronary events by 14% (de Souza 2011).

When dealing with any type of cardiovascular disease, consider adding yarrow to your daily health regimen. Also consider adding herbs like hawthorn (*Crataegus oxyacantha* or *monogyna*) flower, leaves and berries, Asian ginseng (*Panax ginseng*) root or American Ginseng (*Panax quinquefolius*) root, as well generous amounts of garlic (*Allium sativum*) to your diet.

Yarrow and the reproductive system

Herbalists have long considered yarrow a universal regulator of female reproductive function (Holmes 1989, Trickey 1998). By stimulating the return of blood via the venous system, it helps reduce and eliminate uterine and pelvic congestion. It has been used for menstrual problems, including abnormal bleeding problems, menstrual irregularities, excessive menstruation (sometimes used as a sitz bath), as well as prostate inflammation in males. One of the best uterine astringents used to treat menorrhagia (menstrual bleeding that is heavy or that lasts more than a few days) is yarrow. On one hand, it relieves delayed painful menses and allays painful menstruation. On the other hand, it is used as a hemostatic (stops blood flow) remedy to stop excessive bleeding when taken long term (Stansbury, vol. 3, 2018). Yarrow contains tannins, constituents that make this plant a useful astringent. Its ability to stop gynecological bleeding is thought to be related to other constituents such as the flavonoids and an alkaloid called achilleine (Mills 1991). Yarrow is often combined with one or more uterine tonic herbs to normalize uterine function (Trickey 1998). It excels when used in combination with other uterine tonic herbs such as shatavari (*Asparagus racemosus*) root (Pole 2006), dong quai (*Angelica sinensis*) root (Bone 1996), or red raspberry (*Rubus idaeus*) leaf (Trickey 1998). Yarrow can be used in the treatment of painful, cramp-like conditions of the lower part of the female pelvis as a sitz bath.

I have been using fresh yarrow flower tops successfully for many years for prostate inflammation. I also include other herbs such as fresh saw palmetto (*Serenoa repens*) berry, dong quai (*Angelica sinensis*) root, and fresh stinging nettle (*Urtica dioica*) root. Yarrow is excellent to decrease inflammation of the reproductive and urinary tract mucous membranes in both sexes.

Yarrow root and toothache

Both Uphof (1968) and Moerman (1995) report that many Native American tribes used yarrow root to relieve toothaches. Here in the Southwestern United States, various Tewa-speaking Pueblo natives have chewed on or made the tea from the roots to treat toothaches (Dunmire 1995). The root has been shown to contain the constituent eugenol, known as a local anesthetic agent. Chewing the root releases this compound which reduces or stops toothache pain.

Yarrow root is effective for sore gums or teeth, says Michael Moore (2003). He suggests that the root should be chewed for this purpose and/or the tincture of the root applied topically. In his inimitable way of writing about herbs, Michael describes coming across a jar of yarrow roots soaking in brandy in a depression-era glass canning jar in a store of the small town called Oark, deep in Arkansas. He writes that the town was named Oark because "the printer had no Zs left when he printed up the town papers" Michael tried yarrow root for his sore tooth and found that it was effective against the pain (Moore 2003).

Yarrow and the nervous system

The English herbalist Thomas Bartram (1998) wrote that yarrow is a gentle relaxant and acts in a similar manner to chamomile (*Matricaria chamomilla*) on the nervous system. Mességué (1975) used yarrow in nervous afflictions that were resistant to treatment with other herbs. He recommended a tea made with one tablespoon of the dried flower tops per cup of boiling water. He advised not to make more than a cupful at a time, as the tea will darken considerably over a few hours and deteriorate under light. When used for nervous system issues, Mességué suggested adding lemon balm (*Melissa officinalis*) leaves and a pinch of chamomile (*Matricaria chamomilla*) flowers to the yarrow infusion for additional nervous system support.

How to Use Yarrow as Medicine

Internally: Make tea from the recently dried herb; 1 to 2 teaspoon(s) to each cup of boiling water. Use one wine glassful to one cupful three to four times a day (Hutchens 1973). If fresh, use 2 to 4 tablespoons for each cup of boiling water. Let it sit/infuse for 5 minutes, covered. Filter. Use 1 cup three to four times a day.

For yarrow tincture, use 2 to 4 ml of the extract (Duke 2002).

Yarrow herbal extract made with 50% alcohol: Take 10 to 40 drops three times a day (morning, noon, and night) 20 minutes before meals (Moore 1990).

Externally: Infuse two teaspoons of fresh or dry yarrow flowering tops per cup of hot water for 10 minutes. Use as a compress for skin diseases of all kinds, as well as for hemorrhoids (Valnet 1992).

Yarrow baths can be prepared to lessen pain and inflammation. Use a handful of the dried or fresh flowers or leaves in 1 pint (500 ml) of boiling water, let it infuse for 15 minutes, strain to remove the herb, and add the strained liquid to the bath water (Bartram 1998).

Safety: There are no safety concerns surrounding the use of this herb. The *Botanical Safety Handbook* classifies yarrow as a **Safety Class 1** herb, an herb that can be safely consumed when used appropriately (Gardner 2013).

Pregnancy and Lactation: No information on the safety of yarrow during pregnancy and lactation has been identified (Gardner 2013). One animal study showed a decrease in fetal weight in offspring of rats administered high (2.8 g/kg) doses of yarrow, but no adverse effects were seen at lower doses (Boswell-Ruys 2003). However, Applequist (2011) reviewed the study and suggested that Boswell-Ruys et al. failed to correctly interpret their own data. Applequist concluded by saying that "There was, in short, no evidence that yarrow has any independent effect whatsoever on fetal development" (Applequist 2011).

The authors of *Botanical Safety Handbook* note that while their review did not identify any concerns for use of yarrow during pregnancy or while nursing, it does not mean that safety has been conclusively established (Gardner 2013).

Contraindications: None known (Gardner 2013).

Adverse Effects and Side Effects: There have been confirmed reports of contact allergy to yarrow (Gardner 2013). Scientists believed that yarrow's contact allergy is caused by a compound found in the plant called sesquiterpene lactone, specifically α-peroxyachifolid (Hausen 1996).

Drug Interactions: The *Botanical Safety Handbook* has classified yarrow as an **Interaction Class A** herb, "an herb for which no clinically relevant interactions are expected" (Gardner 2013).

Achillea millefolium L. Sturm, J. *Deutschlands flora*, 1801.
Public Domain, plantillustrations.org

References

Abdel-Rahman, RF., Alqasoumi, SI.., El-Desoky, AH., Soliman, GA., Paré, PW., Hezagy, EF. 2015. "Evaluation of the anti-inflammatory, analgesic and anti-ulcerogenic potentials of *Achillea fragrantissima* (Forssk.)." *South African Journal of Botany* 98: 122-127.

Albert-Puleo, M. 1978. "Mythobotany, pharmacology, and chemistry of thujone-containing plants and derivatives." *Economic Botany,* 32(1): 65–74.

Ali, S. I., Gopalakrishnan, B., & Venkatesalu, V. (2017). "Pharmacognosy, Phytochemistry and Pharmacological Properties of *Achillea millefolium* L.: A Review." *Phytotherapy Research.* 31(8): 1140–1161.

Applequist, WL., & Moerman, DE. (2011). "Yarrow *(Achillea millefolium L.):* A Neglected Panacea? A Review of Ethnobotany, Bioactivity, and Biomedical Research." *Economic Botany.* 65 (2): 209–225.

Arnold, WN. 1989. "Absinthe." *Scientific American.* 260(6): 112–117.

Bakun, P., Czarczynska-Goslinska, B., and Goslinski, T. and Lijewski, S. (2021). "In vitro and in vivo biological activities of azulene derivatives with potential applications in medicine." *Medicinal Chemistry Research.* 30: 834-846.

Bartram, T. (1998). *Bartram's Encyclopedia of Herbal Medicine.* Constable and Robinson Ltd.

Benedek, B., and Kopp, B. 2007. "*Achillea millefolium* L. s.l. revisited: Recent findings confirm the traditional use." *Wiener Medizinische Wochenschrift,* 157(13-14): 312–314.

Benedek, B., Geisz, N., Jäger, W., Thalhammer, T., and Kopp, B. 2006. "Choleretic effects of yarrow *(Achillea millefolium* s.l.) in the isolated perfused rat liver." *Phytomedicine.* 13(9-10): 702–706.

Bone, K. 1996. *Clinical Applications of Ayurvedic and Chinese Herbs.* Phytotherapy Press.

Bone, K. 2003. *A Clinical Guide to Blending Liquid Herbs.* Elsevier Churchill Livingstone.

Boswell-Ruys, CL., Ritchie, HE., and Brown-Woodman, PD. (2003). "Preliminary screening study of reproductive outcomes after exposure to yarrow in the pregnant rat." *Birth Defects Research Part B: Developmental and Reproductive Toxicology.* 68 (5): 416–420.

British Herbal Compendium. 1983. British Herbal Medical Association.

Cavalcanti, AM., Baggio, CH., Freitas, CS., Rieck, L., de Sousa, RS., Da Silva-Santos, JE., Mesia-Vela, S., and Marques, MCA. 2006. "Safety and antiulcer efficacy studies of *Achillea millefolium* L. after chronic treatment in Wistar rats." *J. Ethnopharmacol.* 107(2): 277-284.

Chandler, RF., Hooper, SN., and Harvey, MJ. 1982. "Ethnobotany and phytochemistry of yarrow, *Achillea millefolium,* Compositae." *Economic Botany.* 36(2): 203–223.

Choudhary, MI., Jalil, S., Todorova, M., Trendfilova, A., Mikhova, B., Duddeck, H., Rahman, A. 2007. "Inhibitory effect of lactone fractions and individual components from three species of the *Achillea millefolium* complex of Bulgarian origin on the human neutrophils respiratory burst activity." *Natural Product Research: Formerly Natural Product Letters,* 21(11): 1032-1036,

de Souza, P., Gasparotto, A., Crestani, S., Stefanello, MÉA., Marques, MCA., Silva-Santos, JE., and Kassuya, CAL. 2011. "Hypotensive mechanism of the extracts and artemetin isolated from *Achillea millefolium* L. (Asteraceae) in rats." *Phytomedicine,* 18(10): 819–825.

Duke, J. 1985. *Handbook of Medicinal Herbs.* CRC Press.

Duke, J. 2002. *Handbook of Medicinal Herbs.* CRC Press.

Dunmire, WW. and Tierney, GD. 1995. *Wild Plants of the Pueblo Province.* Museum of New Mexico Press.

Ehrendorfer, F. and Guo, YP. 2006. "Multidisciplinary Studies on *Achillea* sensu lato (*Compositae-Anthemideae*): New Data on Systematics and Phylogeography." *Willdenowia* Bd. 36, H. 1, Special Issue: Festschrift Werner Greuter. 36: 69-87.

Foster, S. 1993. *Herbal Renaissance.* Gibbs-Smith Publisher.

Fournier, P. 1948. *Le livre des plantes médicinales et vénéneuses de France.* Tome 1. Paris, France : Editions Lechevalier.

Gardner, Z. and McGuffin, M. editors. 2013. *Botanical Safety Handbook,* 2 ed. CRC Press.

Grieve, M. 1971. *A Modern Herbal.* Dover Publications, Inc. (reprint of 1931 ed.).

Hardy, K., Buckley, S., and Huffman, M. 2016. "Doctors, chefs or hominin animals? Non-edible plants and Neanderthals." *Antiquity.* 90(353): 1373–1379.

Hausen, B. 1996. "A 6-year experience with Compositae mix." *American Journal of Contact Dermatitis,* 7 (2): 94–99.

Holmes, P. 1989. *The Energetic of Western Herbs.* Artemis Press.

Hoffmann, D. 1983. *The New Holistic Herbal*. Element Books Limited.

Hoffmann, D. 2003. *Medical Herbalism*. Healing Arts Press.

Huang, K.C. 1993. *The Pharmacology of Chinese Herbs*. CRC Press.

Hutchens, AR. 1973. *Indian Herbology of North America*. Merco.

Khan, A., & Gilani, A. H. 2011. "Blood pressure lowering, cardiovascular inhibitory and bronchodilatory actions of *Achillea millefolium*." *Phytotherapy Research*, 25(4): 577–583.

Kundakovic, T., Dobric, S., Bokonjic, D., Dragojevic-Simic, V., Kilibarda, V. and Kovacevic, N. 2000. "Anti-inflammatory and anti-ulcer activity of *Achillea alexandri-regis*." *Pharmazie*. 55 (11): 866-867.

Lachenmeier, DW., Emmert, J., Kuballa, T., and Sartor, G. (2006). "Thujone—Cause of absinthism?" *Forensic Science International*. 158 (1): 1–8.

Leclerc, H. 1976. *Précis de phytothérapie*. 5 ed. Masson. (First published in 1922).

Lemmens-Gruber, R., Marchart, E., Rawnduzi, P., Engel, N., Benedek, B., and Kopp, B. (2006). "Investigation of the Spasmolytic Activity of the Flavonoid Fraction of *Achillea millefolium* s.l. on Isolated Guinea-pig Ilea." *Arzneimittelforschung*. 56(08): 582–588.

Leung, A. and S. Foster. 1996. *Encyclopedia of Common Natural Ingredients used in Food, Drugs and Cosmetics*. 2 ed. John Wiley & Sons, Inc.

Menzies-Trull, C. 2003. *Herbal Medicine, Keys to Physiomedicalism including Pharmacopoeia*. Faculty of Physiomedical Herbal Medicine.

Mességué, M. 1975. *Mon herbier de santé*. Laffont.

Mills, S. 1991. *Out of the Earth*. Viking Arcana.

Moerman, DE. 1998. *Native American Ethnobotany*. Timber Press.

Moore, M. 1990. *Herbal Materia Medica*. Silver City, NM Southwest School of Botanical Medicine.

Moore, M. 2003. *Medicinal Plants of the Mountain West*. Revised and expanded edition. Museum of New Mexico Press.

Navarro-Núñez, L., Lozano, M. L., Palomo, M., Martínez, C., Vicente, V., Castillo, J., … Rivera, J. (2008). "Apigenin Inhibits Platelet Adhesion and Thrombus Formation and Synergizes with Aspirin in the Suppression of the Arachidonic Acid Pathway." *Journal of Agricultural and Food Chemistry, 56(9), 2970–2976.*

Nickell, JM. (1976). *J.M. Nickell's Botanical Ready Reference*. CSA Press.

Padosch, A., Lanchemeier, DW. And Kroner, LU. 2006. "Absinthism: A fictious 19th century syndrome with present impact." *Substance Abuse Treatment, Prevention, and Policy*. 1:14

Pole, S. 2006. *Ayurvedic Medicine: The Principles of Traditional Practice*. Churchill Livingstone Elsevier.

Priest, AW. and Priest, LR. 1983. *Herbal Medication*. The C.W. Daniel Company Ltd.

Schilcher, H. 1997. *Phytotherapy in Paediatrics. Handbook for Physicians and Pharmacists*. 2 ed. Medpharm Scientific Publishers.

Sen, T. 2020. Losar, Gandan. Department of Environment, Science & Technology. Government of Himachal Pradesh, India. Available at: https://himalayanwildfoodplants.com/2020/06/achillea-millefolium-l-losar-%E0%A4%B2%E0%A5%8B%E0%A4%B8%E0%A4%B0-gandan/. Accessed on 8/29/2023.

Shah, R., and Peethambaran, B. 2018. "Anti-inflammatory and Anti-microbial Properties of *Achillea millefolium* in Acne Treatment." *Immunity and Inflammation in Health and Disease,* 241–248.

Skenderi, G. 2003. *Herbal Vade Mecum*. Herbacy Press.

Stansbury, J. 2018. *Herbal Formularies for Health Professionals Vol. 3. Endocrinology*. Chelsea Green Publishing.

Tadić, V., Arsić, I., Zvezdanović, J., Zugić, A., Cvetković, D., and Pavkov, S. (2017). "The estimation of the traditionally used yarrow *(Achillea millefolium* L. Asteraceae*)* oil extracts with anti-inflammatory potential in topical application.*" Journal of Ethnopharmacology*. 199: 138–148.

Trickey, R. 1998. *Women, Hormones & Menstrual Cycle*. Allen & Unwin.

Uphof, J.C. 1968. *Dictionary of Economic Plants*. Stechert-Harner Service Agency, Inc.

Valnet, J. 1992. *Phytothérapie*. 6 ed. Maloine.

Van Hellemont, J. 1986. *Compendium de Phytothérapie*. Association Pharmaceutique Belge.

Villalva, M., Jaime, L., Siles-Sánchez, MdlN., and Santoyo, S. 2022. "Bioavailability Assessment of Yarrow Phenolic Compounds Using an In Vitro Digestion/Caco-2 Cell Model: Anti-Inflammatory Activity of Basolateral Fraction." *Molecules*. 27, 8254.

Wichtl, M. (Ed.) 2004. *Herbal Drugs and Phytopharmaceuticals*. 3 ed. CRC Press.

Willard, T. 1992. *Edible and Medicinal Plants of the Rocky Mountains and Neighbouring Territories.* Wild Rose College of Natural Healing, Ltd.

Wren, RB. 1988. *Potter's New Cyclopaedia of Botanical Drugs and Preparations.* Revised by E. Williamson. The C.W. Daniel Company Limited.

Yaeesh, S., Jamal, Q., Khan, A., and Gilani, A. H. 2006. "Studies on hepatoprotective, antispasmodic and calcium antagonist activities of the aqueous-methanol extract of *Achillea millefolium." Phytotherapy Research.* 20(7): 546–551.

Zimmermann, M., Johnson, H., McGuffin, M. and Applequist, W. 2023. *AHPA's Herbs of Commerce*, 3 ed. American Herbal Products Association.

Daniel Gagnon, Medical Herbalist, MS, RH (AHG) is a French-Canadian originally from Northern Ontario who relocated to Santa Fe, NM, in 1979. He has been a practicing Medical Herbalist since 1976. Daniel is the author of *The Practical Guide to Herbal Medicines*, a book designed to provide herbal health care options. With Amadea Morningstar, he is also the co-author of *Breathe Free*, a book on healing the respiratory system. He regularly teaches herbal therapeutics both nationally and internationally. For over 40 years, Daniel has been the owner of Herbs, Etc., an herbal medicine retail store and manufacturing facility located in Santa Fe. www.herbsetc.com. Daniel can be reached at botandan@aol.com.

The feathery foliage of yarrow dries quickly and should be stored in jars. *Susan Belsinger*

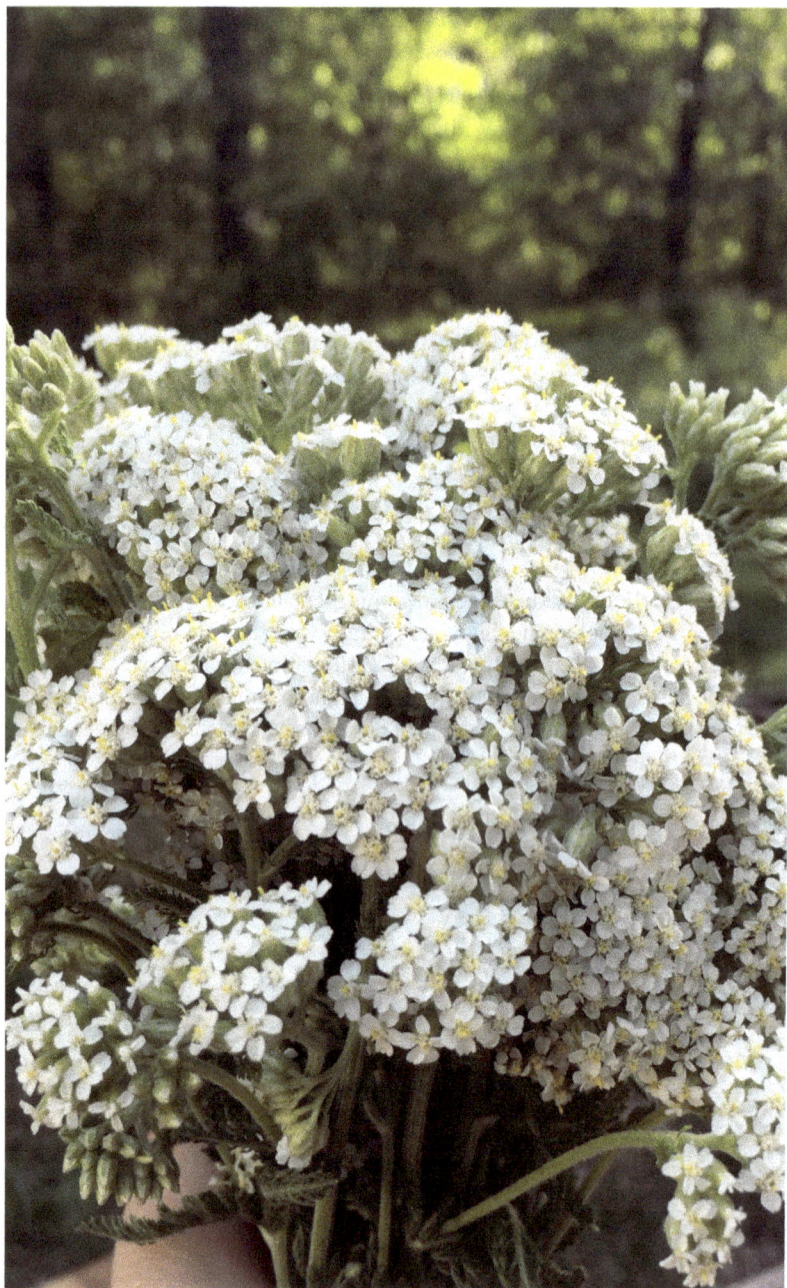

Bouquet of yarrow. *Heather Cohen*

Yarrow in the Apothecary

Carol Little R.H.

Such an ancient plant is yarrow, with her feathery leaves and delicate flowers. Don't let appearances fool you. This sweet, whimsical herb is a powerful green ally and treasured by every herbalist for her wide range of healing attributes.

In June, years ago, on a road trip home from the International Herb Symposium near Boston, I was thrilled to be given an entire bouquet of yarrow by my dear friends, Matthias and Andrea Reisen, from Healing Spirits Herb Farm in New York State. Funny isn't it? I would rather receive a gift of fresh lovingly grown and harvested yarrow, than a trip to any mall.

In my apothecary, yarrow is used in tinctures, teas, infused oil and powdered form. Yarrow has many uses, in various body systems. Although often thought of for wound healing and fever treatment, yarrow offers so much more.

There are times when yarrow is a must and calls my name to be a part of a healing formula. Yarrow has a wide range of chemical constituents so its effects are very diverse. We can use yarrow in so many ways as herbalists, at home, and in clinic.

Typically, we harvest the top 20 to 30 percent of the plant, early in its flowering period, late June to mid-July in southern Ontario

Some of the most common and revered properties of yarrow herb include antiallergenic, antibacterial, anticatarrhal, anti-inflammatory, antirheumatic, antispasmodic, antiulcerogenic, antiviral, appetite stimulant, astringent, bitter, carminative, cholagogue, depurative, diaphoretic, emmenagogue (stimulating), febrifuge, hemostatic/styptic, hypotensive, sialagogue, stomachic, vascular tonic, vasodilator (neural, peripheral), and vulnerary.

Also, to a lesser degree, this amazing herb can be analgesic, antifungal,

A tea made from yarrow flowers and leaves is one of the simplest ways to benefit from this herb's medicinal properties. *Susan Belsinger*

antithrombotic, choleretic, diuretic, expectorant, hypoglycemic, immune stimulant, lymphatic, relaxant, and tranquilizer.

From the dozens of attributes above, we see that our special friend, yarrow, can be a tremendous help and healer for many health issues. There are so many applications and uses.

Here are some ideas, for the home herbalist or the clinician:

Yarrow is a mild tranquilizer and can help to support us in stressful times.

Yarrow is noted to be helpful treating inflammatory conditions of all types, including more serious conditions like atherosclerosis. It can be used to heal gingivitis, mouth ulcers, sore throats, gastric and duodenal ulcers—in fact the entire digestive tract!

Yarrow is an excellent herb to use in cases of digestive distress or imbalance. We can use it for poor digestion and/or appetite, anorexia, colitis, diarrhea, IBS (irritable bowel syndrome) or ulcers. The leaves and flowers have both a pungent and bitter taste, which stimulate the digestive system and relieve liver and gall bladder congestion. It is believed to increase digestive secretions, which can help to relieve painful bloating and gas, as well as both acute and chronic indigestion. It's important to note that one needs to actually taste the bitter flavour in this case, for a good result.

We can use yarrow effectively to reduce fevers. It is commonly used for the flu, fevers and colds when accompanied by fevers as well as chickenpox, measles, and mumps. We can also choose yarrow for upper respiratory infections with watery catarrh. It's excellent for runny nose, allergy symptoms, head colds and sinusitis.

Herbal Tea for Fevers

When treating a fever, serve this tea warm. I learned this classic herbal tea formula from Rosemary Gladstar, years ago. It is very effective. This tea doesn't taste great, but it lowers the fever, makes one sweat, eases headaches and joint pain and helps to fight off infection. This blend is excellent for both children and adults. Make a big batch to have on hand, and you'll be ready.

Yarrow flowers and/or leaves
Spearmint leaves
Elderflowers

Mix equal parts of the yarrow, spearmint and elderflowers to total 1 tablespoon dried, or 2 tablespoons fresh. Place in a glass canning jar. Add 1 cup of just boiled water, cover with lid and steep for 8 to 10 minutes. Strain. Add some maple syrup or honey.

Drink 1/4 to 1/2 cup frequently, at least every hour.

Yarrow is one of the best herbs for vascular conditions, as it is a good vascular tonic. We use it for bruising, edema, damage to blood vessels, hemorrhoids and other inflammatory conditions of the blood and lymphatic vessels. It can be a successful part of a program to repair varicose veins.

Yarrow can be an amazing remedy for circulatory issues, as it improves peripheral circulation. When used in acute protocols for hypertension, it can help cause a temporary drop in blood pressure. It can be a beneficial addition to formulae for cardiovascular conditions.

Yarrow's anti-inflammatory properties make it an excellent supporter of the urinary system. We often combine it with strong diuretics in this case.

We can use the powers of yarrow to assist with female reproductive tract conditions. It is used for bloating, edema, cramps, amenorrhea (absence of menses), or menorrhagia (excessive bleeding). I have used yarrow successfully to treat stomach cramps and menstrual cramps. Painful periods with severe bloating and edema can be relieved, in many cases. Since yarrow is a mild tranquilizer, it can be calming, while acting as an anti-spasmodic cramp reliever.

Yarrow is a great epithelial herb and as such is useful for cuts, bites, and stings. It is very healing when used for soft tissue injuries such as bruises, strains, and sprains. For optimum results when used topically it can be combined with a rubefacient (herbs that can relieve pain and enhance blood circulation). The antibacterial properties plus powerful astringency can help to promote rapid healing.

Infusing yarrow in olive oil makes the foundation for a very healing salve. I have made many, using yarrow alone or in tandem with plantain, comfrey, and Saint John's Wort. Many nourishing herbs can combine to make glorious salves!

Yarrow can be a lifesaver in wound management. It helps with bleeding, both internal and external. The astringent properties help to reduce swelling in external wounds. Make a poultice from the fresh leaves for bruised areas, or make a tea from dried yarrow and use a clean cloth to apply it as a poultice. Yarrow can stop bleeding and makes an excellent styptic. Since it is also anti-inflammatory, pain-relieving, antimicrobial, and wound healing, it is a good choice for shaving cuts, skinned knees, bleeding mosquito bites, and other minor wounds. It's a great idea to have dried or powdered yarrow in a first aid kit so that it can be used as needed to stop bleeding.

Styptic Powder

Pick young yarrow leaves, dry them, and grind into a powder.

Store in a small amber or dark glass jar. Pinch the powder out of the jar and apply to areas needing attention.

Yarrow's detoxifying properties can be most useful for chronic skin conditions. It also can be a very good herb for rheumatoid arthritis, gout, and other rheumatic conditions. It helps to eliminate uric acid (which can also be a problem for our kidneys.)

As an anti-allergenic herb, yarrow can be helpful with hay fever symptoms and can be used preventively in a general immune-boosting formula with echinacea or other immune-modulating herbs. It's a good idea to start treatment a few months before symptoms generally appear for best results.

Below are some more ideas for use in clinical formulae: These specifics are from class notes at The Living Earth School of Herbalism.

Michael Vertolli suggests we use yarrow in formulae at 20 to 25 percent. He also shares his favourite synergistic combinations from his many years as a traditional herbalist and formulator:

For fever, influenza and viral infections—yarrow combines well with boneset, wild bergamot, and/or blue vervain.

For upper respiratory infections, allergies and catarrh—yarrow combines well with purple loosestrife, boneset, wild bergamot, garden sage, elder flowers, and echinacea root.

For high blood pressure—yarrow combines well with motherwort, hawthorn berries, and lemon balm.

Toxicity and/or Concerns: There may be a slight risk of increased sensitivity to sunlight in fair-skinned individuals with prolonged use of this herb, though this has not been conclusively demonstrated.

Contraindications: Not recommended during pregnancy or lactation

I've done my best to share some ideas from my own experiences using this powerhouse herbal ally over my own 20+ years in practice in Toronto. I have always loved yarrow and can remember choosing it for a school project long ago. I was both thrilled and dismayed to discover that yarrow had so many healing attributes—the project was probably ten times larger than it may have been if I'd chosen another herb!

The vast range of healing uses for our beloved yarrow make this sweet green sister a definite must for all of us—to study, to embrace, to grow and to use!

This lengthy list of possibilities may be incomplete, as other uses exist for sure, but I hope I have given you some new ideas about how to include lovely yarrow in your life and in your own health journey.

Carol Little, R.H. is a traditional herbalist in Toronto, Canada, where she has had a private practice for the last 20+ years. She loves to write about how we can embrace herbs in our daily lives. Her easy-to-digest weekly blog posts offer quick takeaway ideas to help readers to feel their best. (https://www.studiobotanica.com)

Carol is a current professional and past board member of the Ontario Herbalists Association. She combines her love of travel and passion for all things green and loves to write about both. Carol has written for *Vitality Magazine* for many years. She is a regular contributor to the IHA annual *Herb of the Year* book. She is a proud participant in the much-loved *FIRE CIDER 101 Zesty Recipes for Health-Boosting Remedies* by Rosemary Gladstar and friends.

Carol's current project is a fun-filled "deep dive" into ONE herb each month - it's called HerbGals and it's a creative interactive way to learn about the many gifts and practical ways we can embrace the green world. Herb enthusiasts, herbalists, gardeners, or those with culinary interests are sharing and learning from each other!

For more information:
https://studiobotanica.teachable.com/p/herbgals
https://www.facebook.com/studiobotanica
https://instagram.com/studiobotanica

Yarrow foliage is easily dried by spreading it out in large, flat, baskets. *Susan Belsinger*

Organic Yarrow Essential Oil. *Dorene Petersen*

Under-Appreciated Yarrow Essential Oil

Dorene Petersen

Beautiful blue yarrow, *Achillea millefolium* L., essential oil is clearly underappreciated given the lack of clinical trials. Fortunately, it is not neglected by many aromatherapists who value its unique phytochemistry and varied therapeutic actions, ranging from antimicrobial and antifungal to anti-inflammatory. These actions are even more valuable given that many microbes and fungi are now multidrug resistant.

Yarrow's Latin name reveals its rich history and leaf shape. The genus *Achillea* was named after Achilles, a legendary warrior in Greek Mythology. It is said he administered poultices of yarrow to treat soldiers' wounds in the battle of Troy.[1] The Latin name *millefolium* means a thousand leaves, hence the common name of milfoil.[2] It belongs to the same family as sunflowers, Asteraceae (formerly Compositae).

Yarrow has a long history of medicinal uses across many diverse cultures. Pliny the Elder and Dioscorides both documented the use of yarrow during the first century C.E.[3] Later, the English herbalist John Gerard (c.1545–1612) also mentions Achilles in his original herbal, *The Generall Historie of Plantes.*[4] Achilles knew his plants, and some of yarrow's common names, nosebleed, and bloodwort, are clues of its use as a styptic herb — an astringent herb powerful enough to halt bleeding.

This potent styptic property also earned it the name *Herba Militaris*, the military herb. Yarrow stalks were and still are important in divination. The ancient yarrow-stalk method is the fundamental divination method used in the *I Ching*.[5 6]

What Species is the Essential Oil Made From?

The genus *Achillea* contains approximately 110 to 140 species.[7] However, the essential oil of yarrow found in commerce is usually produced from *A. millefolium* flowers and leaves, not from the cultivated varieties that can differ in color, flowers, leaves, structure, and pharmacological constituents. The stems are simple, angular, rough, hairy, and erect. They grow to about one to one and a half feet high and are grayish green. The deep green, finely dissected leaves have a feathery appearance. The flowers can be grayish-white or pinkish-red and in a daisy-like cluster with four to six florets. There is also a cultivated yellow variety, but as mentioned above, the white and pink are considered more medicinal and used for essential oil production.[8]

However, while not commonly used, there are several other species found in Turkey, such as *A. setacea, A. teretifoli, A. biebersteinii,* and *A. tenuifolia;* and *A. filipendulina,* found in Sardinia, and Iran. These species produce many constituent variations, and while rare, you may see them in commerce as steam-distilled essential oil.

Because of this variation in yarrow species and to avoid buying an essential oil with a constituent profile unsuitable for the outcome you hope to achieve, always check the Latin name. As mentioned, not all yarrow essential oils are the same. Don't rely on the common name of yarrow or other names you may come across, such as milfoil, thousand leaf, common yarrow, and old man's pepper.

Growing Yarrow for Essential Oil Production

Yarrow is easy to grow both domestically and on a larger scale. It is native to Europe, Northern Asia, and North America. In the United States, it is a common weed in many different habitats: You will see yarrow at the seashore, high desert, and fields; it even grows wild in cities. Yarrow is a perennial herb propagated by seed or division of rhizomes in the spring. It is an adaptable herb and grows well in ordinary garden soil in either sun or shade. While yarrow is easy to grow and seems to grow everywhere, it is not a common or easily obtained essential oil; partially because the yield from steam distillation is so low that the financial return is limited.

How Yarrow Essential Oil is Produced

The oil is steam-distilled from the flowers and some leaves. The highest yield is from semi-dried or dried yarrow flowers. Dried or semi-dried flowers produce about .25 - 50%, while fresh flowers offer .07 - 25% essential oil. You may wonder why fresh or dried makes a difference and what the yield refs to. When you use fresh, there is always water in the plant; you get less plant in the retort and therefore less yield. It also costs more energy to run the still because you have to boil the water in the plant. On the other hand, dry plant material has no water, and you can pack more in the still, giving a higher yield. The yield is the weight of essential oil compared to the weight of plant material. To calculate yield, weigh the plant before distilling, and then at the end, weigh the essential oil—so if you have one hundred pounds of plant and produce 1 pound of oil, your yield is 1%. Yarrow also requires re-distillation as approximately 21% of the oil dissolves in the distillation water and must be re-distilled and added back into the oil.

Steam distillation is preferred because this method produces oil containing the preferred anti-inflammatory constituent, chamazulene, depending on the species. Be aware, however, that not all steam-distilled yarrow oil will contain chamazulene, and a solvent extraction is always devoid of chamazulene. Data on the impact of environment and or altitude on the chamazulene content or overall constituent profile of yarrow is varied. Lawrence states that these influences do not affect the constituent profile [9] We do know that there is much genetic variation in yarrow, which can produce yarrow essential oils lacking any chamazulene. [10]

Chemotypes

Chemotypes impact the chemical profile of yarrow oil. The basis of chemotypes is variation in chemical composition occurring within a genus. Chemotypes are genetic adaptations, so this composition remains largely consistent for that particular plant irrespective of its growing conditions or locale. [11] A 2003 study of yarrow from 21 habitats in Lithuania revealed four distinct chemotype groups, some completely devoid of chamazulene.

Categorizing the four groups revealed:
Group 1: borneol and camphor
Group 2: chamazulene and β-pinene
Group 3: (E)-nerolidol and β-pinene
Group 4: 1,8-cineole and β-pinene [12]

While each of these oils would have wellness benefits, this study reveals how important it is to review the constituent profile of essential oils if you are expecting a specific therapeutic outcome.

As we can see, yarrow's complex genetic makeup and varied species produce different essential oils with different therapeutic outcomes. If you want to

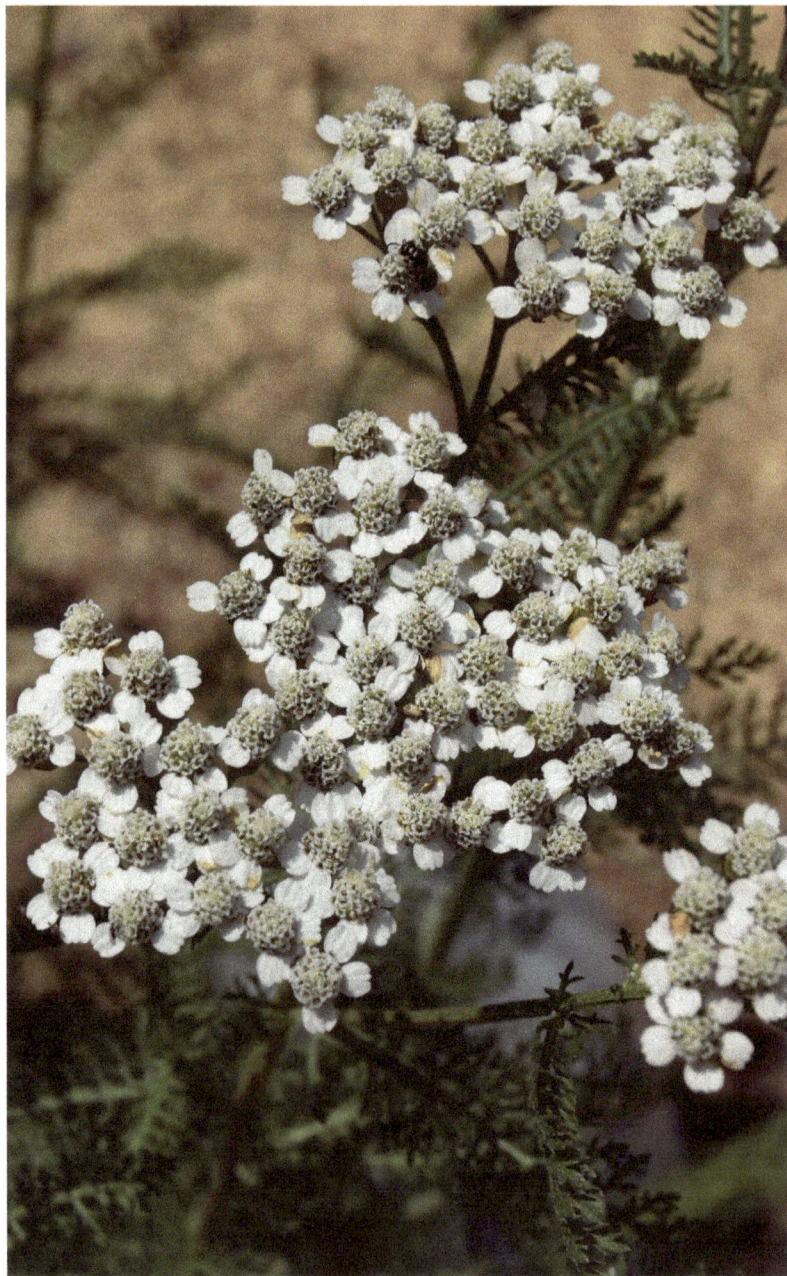

Essential oil of wild white yarrow is distilled from the flowers and some leaves. *Pat Kenny*

use yarrow essential oil for therapeutic actions, know what you are looking for and, ideally, check the gas chromatographic-mass spectrometer analysis (GC/MS). If you want anti-inflammatory action, a yarrow oil with a high (above 45%) chamazulene is most likely to produce results. However, such high chamazulene content is hard to source, so at least ensure the constituent is present.

Become an Organoleptic Expert

Don't worry if you can't access a GC/MS; all is not lost, as the blue color of the yarrow can reveal the chamazulene levels. The blue color can be even more intense than chamomile *Matricaria chamomilla* L., due to the higher chamazulene content. It can range from pale blue to very dark blue.

However, oxidation has occurred if the color of yarrow essential oil is pale green, gray, or black. Yarrow essential oil is very sensitive to heat, light, and oxygen. Exposure to these influences reduces the oil's therapeutic value. Oxidized oils should not be used for therapeutic purposes, as exposure to air can alter the constituent profile and form sensitizing compounds. Skin sensitization can be painful and leave a red and irritated area on the skin. Discontinuing the oil may not resolve the irritation.[13] Research has shown that encapsulating the essential oil provides protection from these influences and improves efficacy.[14] American College of Healthcare Sciences shares a video regarding essential oil storage considerations, how storage can affect quality, and issues such as sensitization. View online at https://www.youtube.com/watch?v=wngxL1RyqHE&t=5s.

However, it is not just the color of yarrow essential oil we should be concerned with. Observing an oil using all of your senses—known as organoleptic testing—reveals clues to the aromatic constituents (once you become an olfactory expert) and the overall quality of an oil. Conduct an organoleptic evaluation using feel, aroma, and visual inspection and by performing a check of the evaporation rate. Experts and professionals also taste a tiny drop of essential oil on the tip of the tongue as part of organoleptic testing. However, this is not recommended for anyone without clinical training in the safe use of essential oils.

Generally, before conducting organoleptic testing, review the contra-indications for the oil and determine that there are no cautions or contraindications.

Diluents and Extenders

Unfortunately, like many industries where the bottom line takes precedence over the quality of the end product, essential oils can be adulterated with harmful diluents and extenders. Diethyl phthalate (DEP) and dipropylene glycol (DPG) are the most harmful diluents.

The European Union only permits these substances in fragrance products where skin contact is minimal. Unfortunately, this is not the case in the United States.

Ethanol and phthalic acid are used to make DEP. It has a bitter and unpleasant taste and can irritate mucous membranes. When absorbed through the skin, it depresses the nervous system, and current research indicates it may also have possible cancer-causing effects.[15] Diethyl phthalate is often found in sandalwood *Santalum album* L., but can be used to stretch many other oils. A simple test for DEP is to put one drop of the oil on the tip of your tongue. If the oil contains DEP, your tongue will feel numb. Note that there are exceptions. Rose oil is one of these exceptions that can numb your tongue and may not necessarily be adulterated. Rather, this is the analgesic action of eugenol naturally found in small quantities in rose.

However, since we don't advocate tasting essential oils as a home user, it is safer to rely on the feel and evaporation rate of an oil.

Essential oils intended for clinical aromatherapy should not contain dipropylene glycol. It is a colorless liquid that gives essential oils a sweet taste. It is linked to skin sensitivity reactions and is absorbed through the skin better than glycerin. There are currently no regulations requiring the label to list DPG or DEP.

Essential oils that contain these chemicals feel different. They tend to feel oily when rubbed between your thumb and first finger and will evaporate more slowly on a perfume strip or blotter.

Inexpensive aroma chemicals that may or may not have an identical fragrance to the essential oil may also be added to extend an oil. Extenders are usually synthetic but may be extracted from a less expensive oil and added to a costly oil that requires a certain constituent level. "Nature identical" usually refers to a chemically synthesized version extender. Nature-identical oils or constituents are not suitable for clinical therapeutic aromatherapy. Being an expensive oil to produce, yarrow is not spared this fate.

Try dropping a few drops on a perfume blotter. Yarrow should leave a dark to pale blue stain and should evaporate or dry out quickly. It should not have an oily feel when rubbed between the fingers.

As you practice organoleptic testing, your senses will sharpen, and you will easily identify DEP and DPG.

Why Use Yarrow Essential Oil

What makes yarrow essential oil such a valuable oil in your medicine cabinet? While the synergetic complexity and combinations of the constituents provide the unique action, it is a powerful exercise to look closer at what specific constituents in yarrow provide its therapeutic value. The profile contains some remarkable constituents with significant therapeutic potential.

Yarrow essential oil is one of the few essential oils with activity against gram-positive and gram-negative microorganisms. Gram-negative organisms have a cell wall that is very difficult to penetrate for antibiotics or essential oils. An essential oil that has this action is a powerful ally. Keep it in the medicine cabinet alongside the antibiotic cream for slow-healing wounds.

Expectorant and Diaphoretic

Recovering from a cold and excessive mucus is supported by yarrow essential oil. Alpha-terpineol and 1,8 cineole are some of the major constituents responsible for these actions. The 1,8 cineole is antimicrobial and mildly expectorant, making it an extremely effective support remedy for the common cold, along with its diaphoretic action. The 1,8 cineole is also responsible for yarrow's ability to reduce the swelling of mucous membranes, loosen mucus, and ease breathing. It has a mild anesthetic action when applied externally. Sipping on yarrow flower and leaf infusion throughout the day while diffusing yarrow essential oil provides further support.

Insect-repellent

1,8 cineole is also toxic to insects, hence the insect-repellent activity of oils that contain this constituent. Interestingly enough, two unique species of yarrow oils, *A. magnifica* and *A. filipendulina,* oils showed strong antimalarial activity against both chloroquine-sensitive and chloroquine-resistant strains of *Plasmodium falciparum*, a particularly deadly form of malaria.[16] As if malaria is not bad enough, we have seen an increase in dengue and zika due to excessive rainfall in areas impacted by climate change.[17] There is an opportunity for an entrepreneur to develop a yarrow essential oil-based insect repellent. With the addition of lemon eucalyptus *Eucalyptus citriodora* (Hook.) and catnip *Nepeta cataria* (L.) essential oils, yarrow would pack a powerful punch against deadly mosquitoes.

Antimicrobial and Antifungal

As mentioned, yarrow essential oil displays activity against gram-positive and gram-negative microorganisms. *In-vitro* studies have demonstrated the antimicrobial activity of yarrow oil against gram-positive *Streptococcus pneumoniae,* which can cause a range of illnesses from sinusitis to ear infections,[18] gram-positive *Clostridium perfringens,* which causes food poisoning, gram-positive *Candida albicans* causing thrush and vaginal yeast infections, gram-positive and antimicrobial resistant *Mycobacterium smegmatis*[19] causing skin and lung infections,[20] gram-negative multi-drug resistant *Acinetobacter lwoffii*[21] that causes gastroenteritis amongst other illnesses, and is also active against multi-drug resistant fungus *Candida krusei.*[22]

Anti-inflammatory

The anti-inflammatory action is thought to be the result of the chamazulene. *In-vitro* studies demonstrated that yarrow oil suppressed the inflammatory responses in mouse leukemic monocyte macrophage cell lines.[23] This anti-inflammatory action makes yarrow essential oil an effective addition to any skin care product line.

Antiseptic and Vulnerary

The terpenes alpha-pinene, beta-pinene, and limonene, coupled with the 1,8 cineole, are all constituents with an antiseptic action range. This could also explain yarrow's reputation as a wound healer or vulnerary. However, no *in-vitro* or *in-vivo* data could be found to support this use of the essential oil. [24]

Antioxidant, Anticancer

The ketones, artemisia, camphor, and thujone, are powerful additions to yarrow's constituent profile. Various studies have indicated that essential oils with high levels of artemisia ketone, camphor, 1,8 cineole, linalool, and borneol frequently feature some important biological functions, such as antioxidant, anti-inflammatory, antimicrobial, and anticancer activities. The study referenced here confirms yarrow essential oil's anti-inflammatory and antioxidant actions.[25]

Chelator and Hepatic

Yarrow herbal extract has a reputation for supporting the liver.[26]

While there is no clinical evidence that yarrow essential oil is beneficial to the liver, there is anecdotal evidence that yarrow oil can saturate the bloodstream and chelate and absorb different kinds of toxic impurities. Could it be that the terpene alcohols, linalool and borneol, esters (including bornyl acetate), sesquiterpenes, caryophyllene and cadinene, formic acid, acetic acid, isovaleric acid, butyric acid, and a sesquiterpene lactone, achilline, found in yarrow oil have the ability to also improve liver function? More research is clearly needed.

Hemostyptic and Astringent

Yarrow's astringent action is particularly recommended for hemorrhoids with bleeding and pain because it acts as a styptic for the blood vessels and nerves of the anal sphincters and is mildly anesthetic. A study using rats did provide some data to support its gastroprotective action and, in particular, the healing action on gastric ulcers. Human trials would need to be conducted.[27]

Yarrow Essential Oil as a Perfume

While yarrow may not be the first essential oil you think of when formulating a perfume, the sweet, fresh, green, somewhat camphor-like aroma is useful in a blend. It evaporates quite slowly, making it a base to middle note and a useful addition to slow down the evaporation, creating that lingering note long after the first whiff has gone. Think of yarrow as an addition to blends that contain any of these oils; Atlas cedarwood *Cedrus atlantica*, bay leaf *Laurus nobilis*, black pepper *Piper nigrum*, bergamot *Citrus aurantium* var. *bergamia*, cajuput *Melaleuca leucadendron* Roman chamomile *Chamaemelum nobile*, clary sage *Salvia sclarea*, cypress *Cupressus sempervirens*, elemi *Canarium luzonicum*, grapefruit *Citrus paradisi*, juniper *Juniperus communis*, lavender *Lavandula angustifolia*, lemon *Citrus limonum*, marjoram *Origanum majorana*, neroli *Citrus aurantium* var. *amara*, rosemary *Salvia rosmarinus* (*Rosmarinus officinalis*), tea tree New Zealand *Leptospermum scoparium*, vetiver *Vetiveria zizanioides*, and ylang ylang *Cananga odorata* var. *genuina*.

Cautions and Contraindications

While yarrow essential oil contains the potentially toxic constituents camphor and thujone, the *Commission E Monographs* lists no known side effects for yarrow and no known drug interactions.[28] The United States Federal Regulations do require that food or beverage products containing yarrow be thujone-free.[29] Yarrow essential oil is not listed on the FDA Generally Recognized as Safe (GRAS) list.[30]

Older texts indicate it is contraindicated for pregnancy due to its emmenagogue and uterine stimulant activity.[31] This refers to the herb, and later studies say this contraindication was based on a single low-quality rat study, the results of which needed to be correctly interpreted. However, reducing if not totally avoiding the use of medicinal products during pregnancy and nursing is of course always prudent.[32]

People who have allergies to members of the Asteraceae family should either avoid its use or immediately cease use should allergic reactions appear, such as itching and inflammatory changes to the skin.

Excessive doses may interfere with anticoagulant, hypo, and hypertensive therapies, and have sedative and diuretic effects.[33]

The essential oil has a toxic rating of II,[34] and a skin patch test is required before applying it to the skin.

Pay attention to these cautions and contraindications when you choose to use yarrow. Once you have performed your due diligence and are assured of the purity and the constituent profile, you can dissolve 1 to 2 drops in the bath. Mix it before adding it to a full bath with whole-fat milk, and give the water a good swirl.

Yarrow Oil in the Medicine Cabinet

Experience yarrow in your home apothecary with these wellness support blends developed over many years of practice.

Normal Blood Pressure Support Blend

Adults: Inhaled via a diffuser.

Cinnamon bark *Cinnamomum zeylanicum* essential oil: 10 drops
Yarrow *Achillea millefolium* essential oil: 10 drops

To prepare, blend the two oils and store them in a dark bottle in a cool location.

To use, shake well and add 2 to 4 drops per 100 ml of water.

Fill your diffuser with the water and plug it into a power source. If you have a candle diffusor, light the candle.

Note: Don't exceed 30-minute intervals when diffusing and diffuse in well-ventilated areas.

Store your cinnamon bark oil, yarrow oil, and any leftover aromatic water in a cool, dark location.

Essential oils for the Sweet Breath Mouthwash. *Dorene Petersen*

Healthy Muscle and Joint Support. *Dorene Petersen*

Sweet Breath Mouthwash

Buddha wood *Eremophila mitchellii* essential oil: 10 drops
Tea tree Australia *Melaleuca alternifolia* essential oil: 5 drops
Tea tree New Zealand *Leptospermum scoparium* essential oil: 5 drops
Yarrow *Achillea millefolium* essential oil: 3 drops
Peppermint *Mentha* x*piperita* essential oil: 3 drops

Mix the oils in a small clean glass jar (or an inert plastic jar) with a tight-fitting lid. Blend the oils and put three to five drops in one-half cup of warm water. Stir thoroughly and use as a mouth rinse once or twice a day. *Do not swallow.*

Healthy Muscle and Joint Support

Bay *Laurus nobilis* essential oil: 4 drops
Lemon *Citrus limonum* essential oil: 3 drops
Chamomile Roman *Chamaemelum nobile* essential oil: 3 drops
Yarrow *Achillea millefolium* essential oil: 6 drops
Sweet Almond *Prunus dulcis* carrier oil: 1 ounce (1% dilution ratio)

Mix the oils in a small clean glass jar (or an inert plastic jar) with a tight-fitting lid. Blend oils, then massage the areas two to three times a day, using 1/4 ounce (7.5 ml) of the blend.

Healthy Digestion Blend

Bergamot *Citrus aurantium* var. *bergamia* essential oil: 4 drops
Chamomile Roman *Chamaemelum nobile* essential oil: 3 drops
Ginger *Zingiber officinale* essential oil: 3 drops
Yarrow *Achillea millefolium* oil: 3 drops
Sweet almond *Prunus dulcis* carrier oil: 1 ounce (1% dilution ratio)

Mix the oils in a small clean glass jar (or an inert plastic jar) with a tight-fitting lid. Blend oils, then, using 1/4 ounce (7.5 ml) of the blend, massage the stomach and intestinal areas in a clockwise direction using small, circular movements.

The sweet, fresh, green, somewhat camphor-like aroma of yarrow essential oil can be useful in perfume blends. *Susan Belsinger*

Smooth Skin Facial Oil

Prepare a small amount of facial oil at a time to ensure it stays fresh.

Chamomile Roman *Chamaemelum nobile* essential oil: 3 drops
Yarrow *Achillea millefolium* essential oil: 3 drops
Camellia *Camellia sinensis* carrier oil: 3 teaspoons (1% dilution ratio)

Mix the oils in a small clean glass jar (or an inert plastic jar) with a tight-fitting lid.

Apply a small amount to a cleansed face and neck nightly using light upward strokes.

Healthy Blood Flow Massage Oil

Cypress *Cupressus sempervirens* essential oil: 12 drops
Lavender *Lavandula angustifolia* essential oil: 10 drops
Yarrow *Achillea millefolium* essential oil: 4 drops
30 ml of carrier oil (3% dilution)

Mix the essential oils and carrier oil in a glass container with a tight-fitting lid.

Use 1 teaspoon (5 ml) of the blend to massage the desired area twice daily.

When practical, it is ideal to keep the legs elevated while massaging.

References

[1]Applequist, W. L. & Moerman, D.E. (2011). "Yarrow (*Achillea millefolium* L.): A neglected panacea? A review of ethnobotany, bioactivity, and biomedical research." *Economic Botany, 65,* 209–225. https://doi.org/10.1007/s12231-011-9154-3.

[2]United States Department of Agriculture. (n.d.). "Plant of the week: Common Yarrow *(Achillea millefolium)."* https://www.fs.usda.gov/wildflowers/plant-of-the-week/achillea_millefolium.shtml.

[3]Applequist, W. L. & Moerman, D.E. (2011). "Yarrow (*Achillea millefolium* L.): A neglected panacea? A review of ethnobotany, bioactivity, and biomedical research." *Economic Botany, 65,* 209–225. https://doi.org/10.1007/s12231-011-9154-3.

[4]Gerard, J. (1545-1612). *The herball or Generall historie of plantes. Gathered by Iohn Gerarde of London Master in Chirurgerie very much enlarged and amended by Thomas Iohnson citizen and apothecarye of London.* Adam Islip Ioice Norton and Richard Whitakers, anno 1633.

[5]Zheng, X. & Cao, Y. (2023). *Big data analyzing the asymmetry of 64 hexagrams based on the Yarrow-stalk method.* 2023081347. https://doi.org/10.20944/preprints202308.1347.v1.

[6]Shaugnessy, E. L. (2022).*The origin and early development of the Zhou changes.* Brill.

[7]Applequist, W. L. & Moerman, D. E. (2011). "Yarrow (Achillea millefolium L.): A neglected panacea? A review of ethnobotany, bioactivity, and biomedical research." *Economic Botany, 65,* 209–225. https://doi.org/10.1007/s12231-011-9154-3.

[8]Ünlü, M., Daferera, D., Dönmez, E., Polissiou, M., Tepe, B., & Sökmen, A. (2002). "Compositions and the in vitro antimicrobial activities of the essential oils of Achillea setacea and Achillea teretifolia (Compositae)." *Journal of Ethnopharmacology, 83*(1-2), 117-121.

[9]Lawrence, B. M. (2010, June 30). "Progress in essential oils: Yarrow oil, spikenard oil, dwarf pine, and mountain pine oils." *Perfume and Flavorist.* https://www.perfumerflavorist.com/fragrance/ingredients/article/21859133/progress-in-essential-oils-yarrow-oil-spikenard-oil-and-dwarf-pine-and-mountain-pine-oils.

[10]Ibid.

[11]Petersen, D. (2022). *AROMA 203: Aromatherapy I* (20th ed). Unpublished Manuscript. American College of Healthcare Sciences.

[12]Ibid.

[13]Petersen, D. (2020). *Aromatherapy Materia Medica: Essential oil monographs* (20th ed). Unpublished Manuscript. American College of Healthcare Sciences. AROMA 303 textbook.

[14]Rakmai, J., Cheirsilp, B., Torrado-Agrasar, A., Simal-Gándara, J., & Mejuto, J. C. (2017). "Encapsulation of yarrow essential oil in hydroxypropyl-beta-cyclodextrin: physiochemical characterization and evaluation of bio-efficacies." *CyTA-Journal of Food, 15*(3), 409-417. https://doi.org/10.1080/19476337.2017.1286523.

[15]López-Carrillo, L., Hernández-Ramírez, R. U., Calafat, A. M., Torres-Sánchez, L., Galván-Portillo, M., Needham, L. L., & Cebrián, M. E. (2010). "Exposure to phthalates and breast cancer risk in northern Mexico." *Environmental health perspectives, 118*(4), 539-544. https://doi.org/10.1289/ehp.0901091.

[16]Demirci, B., Başer, K., Aytaç, Z., Khan, S. I., Jacob, M. R., & Tabanca, N. (2018). "Comparative study of three *Achillea* essential oils from Eastern part of Turkey and their biological activities." *Records of Natural Products, 12*(2), 195-200. https://www.acgpubs.org/doc/2018073100404809-RNP-EO-1703-019.pdf.

[17]World Health Organization. (n.d.). *Dengue – the region of the Americas.* World Health Organization. https://www.who.int/emergencies/disease-outbreak-news/item/2023-DON475#:~:text=However%2C%20during%20the%20seasonal%20period,of%20historical%20areas%20of%20transmission.

[18]Centers for Disease Control and Prevention. (2020, September 1). "Types of pneumococcal disease. Centers for Disease Control and Prevention." https://www.cdc.gov/pneumococcal/about/infection-types.html.

[19]Seniya, S. P., & Jain, V. (2022). "Decoding phage resistance by mpr and its role in survivability of Mycobacterium smegmatis." *Nucleic acids research, 50*(12), 6938–6952. https://doi.org/10.1093/nar/gkac505.

[20]Wang, C.J., Song, Y., Li, T., Hu, J., Chen, X., & Li, H. "Mycobacterium smegmatis skin infection following cosmetic procedures: Report of two cases." *Clinical, Cosmetic and Investigational Journal*, 15, 535-540.

[21]Elham, B., & Fawzia, A. (2019). "Colistin resistance in Acinetobacter baumannii isolated from critically ill patients: clinical characteristics, antimicrobial susceptibility and outcome." *African Health Sciences, 19*(3), 2400-2406.

[22]Candan, F., Unlu, M., Tepe, B., Daferera, D., Polissiou, M., Sökmen,

A., & Akpulat, H. A. (2003). "Antioxidant and antimicrobial activity of the essential oil and methanol extracts of *Achillea millefolium* subsp. millefolium Afan.(Asteraceae)." *Journal of ethnopharmacology, 87*(2-3), 215-220.

[23]Chou, S. T., Peng, H. Y., Hsu, J. C., Lin, C. C., & Shih, Y. (2013). "*Achillea millefolium* L. essential oil inhibits LPS-induced oxidative stress and nitric oxide production in RAW 264.7 macrophages." *International Journal of Molecular Sciences, 14*(7), 12978-12993.

[24]Vitale, S., Colanero, S., Placidi, M., Di Emidio, G., Tatone, C., Amicarelli, F., & D'Alessandro, A. M. (2022). "Phytochemistry and biological activity of medicinal plants in wound healing: an overview of current research." *Molecules, 27*(11), 3566. https://www.ncbi.nlm.nih.gov/pmc/articles/PMC9182061/.

[25]Chou, S. T., Peng, H. Y., Hsu, J. C., Lin, C. C., & Shih, Y. (2013). "*Achillea millefolium* L. essential oil inhibits LPS-induced oxidative stress and nitric oxide production in RAW 264.7 macrophages." *International journal of molecular sciences, 14*(7), 12978-12993.

[26]Benedek, B., Geisz, N., Jäger, W., Thalhammer, T., & Kopp, B. (2006). "Choleretic effects of yarrow (*Achillea millefolium* sl) in the isolated perfused rat liver." *Phytomedicine, 13*(9-10), 702-706.

[27]Hadavi-Siahboomi, M., Yegdaneh, A., Talebi, A., & Minaiyan, M. (2022). "Ulcer-healing effect of hydroalcoholic extract and essential oil of *Achillea millefolium* L. on murine model of colitis." *International Journal of Preventive Medicine, 13*,155. https://doi.org/10.4103/ijpvm.ijpvm_50_22.

[28]Blumenthal, M. (Ed.). (1998). *The complete German commission e monographs: Therapeutic guide to herbal medicines.* American Botanical Council.

[29]McGuffin, M., Hobbs, C., Upton, R., & Goldberg, A. (Eds.). (1997). *American herbal products association's botanical safety handbook.* CRC Press.

[30]U.S. Food & Drug Administration. (n.d.). CFR-Code of federal regulations title 21. Retrieved September 13, 2013. http://www.accessdata.fda.gov/scripts/cdrh/cfdocs/cfcfr/CFRSearch.cfm?fr=182.20.

[31]McGuffin, M., Hobbs, C., Upton, R., & Goldberg, A. (Eds.). (1997). *American herbal products association's botanical safety handbook.* CRC Press.

[32]Applequist, W. L. & Moerman, D.E. (2011). "Yarrow (*Achillea millefolium* L.): A neglected panacea? A review of ethnobotany, bioactivity,

and biomedical research." *Economic Botany,* 65, 209–225. https://doi.org/10.1007/s12231-011-9154-3.

[33]Newall, C.A., Anderson, L.A., & Philpson, J.D. (1996). *Herbal medicine: A guide for healthcare professionals*. The Pharmaceutical Press.

[34]American College of Healthcare Sciences Toxicity Rating: I = Low, II = Moderate, III = High (Low Therapeutic Margin).

Dorene Petersen BA, DIP.NT, DIP.ACU, RH (AHG) is a New Zealand-trained Naturopath and aromatherapy, herbalism, and holistic wellness expert with decades of experience. Dorene grew up in New Zealand, loving plants, cooking from scratch, and learning to make herbal medicines. She founded the American College of Healthcare Sciences (ACHS) in 1978. During that time, she authored twenty textbooks, (which she continues to edit in her role as Founding President), amongst many other things and continues to write. Her most immense joy is celebrating the successes of ACHS students and graduates and writing and sharing wellness tips. She is now retired as the President of ACHS.edu and lives part-time in Mexico. Contact Dorene at dorenepetersen@achs.edu.

Medieval illustration of the distillation of herbs. *Public Domain, Wellcome Collection.*

Ornamental yellow yarrows, Buffalo Springs Herb Farm, Raphine, Virginia.
Susan Belsinger

Why *Achillea* as Herb of the Year?

Chuck Voigt

The original concept of the Herb of the Year (HOY) promotion of the International Herb Association was to educate people about and to highlight some of the lesser-known herbs. The thought was that by doing this, these herbs could become better understood and more widely utilized. This began in 1995 with the selection of Fennel (genus *Foeniculum*) to be the first herb so honored.

Several criteria were used to determine whether an herb was useful enough to be chosen. Three of the main features required were culinary, medicinal, and decorative. Others might include herbal dye plants, herbal landscapes, and cut flowers or foliage. Usually, those selected have excelled in at least two of the first three traits, and many have also checked some or all of the other boxes as well.

Over the years, the concept has been modified somewhat, including many of the best known herbs in the promotion. The original one or two-page news releases have grown into full-fledged, full-color books, some over 200 pages. The Horticulture Committee has tried to maintain some of the original intent, by mixing in some lesser-known genera with those widely known and used. An informal alternating year format has been developed to that end.

Therein lies a bit of a rub. Culinary usage is clearly the number one entry portal to the world of herbs for most people. Occasionally, herbs have been chosen which have almost no known culinary usage, but which are extremely useful medicinally and ornamentally. Echinacea was the first of these to cause comment among those whose first thoughts about herbs involve edible recipes. Admittedly, there have been only a few which fall into this category, but they have challenged contributors to explore those other attributes in detail, almost always with surprisingly positive results.

Another example of an Herb of the Year which initially met considerable resistance before its selection is Horseradish (genus *Armoracia*). It was thought about in a very narrow window as a condiment for seafood and beef. The surprising result of delving further into this ancient herbal plant was extremely illuminating, yielding a unique and in-depth HOY book. The annual conference held in the commercial growing area of this crop in southwestern Illinois opened the eyes of the attendees. The trip up the learning curve was thrilling, even allowing the viewing of a catsup bottle-shaped water tower in nearby Collinsville, Illinois.

The selection of *Achillea* as the Herb of the Year for 2024 has generated some of the same uncertainty. Admittedly, this genus has limited usage in cooking. It does, however, have an ancient history as a medicinal plant, as well as some fast-developing uses in landscapes, and as fresh and dried floral arrangements, which come into and go out of popularity in cycles. *Achillea* was chosen to offset other, more mainstream choices in surrounding years. It presents a steeper learning curve than many of these others, but that is true to the original concept of the IHA Herb of the Year promotions.

.

As I grew up on my family's northeastern Illinois farm, I would sometimes find myself sitting on a large erratic boulder in the virgin pasture. As the wild but curious beef cattle gradually sidled nearer to me, I was struck by the aromas emanating from the munched plants next to where I was sitting. Among these was *Achillea millefolium*, and to this day, the scent of *Achillea* takes me back to that pasture, which now only remains in memory, since it was turned into corn and soybean fields by others.

As a state horticulture specialist at the University of Illinois, I re-discovered *A. millefolium*, and also many bold new cultivars, starting with basic pastel colors, then blossoming into bolder single-color selections. I came into contact with talented floral designers, such as Don Haynie of Virginia, and came to know the related 'Coronation Gold' cultivar, very useful in fresh and dried arrangements. It also triggered a memory of my high school buddy, who went on to study architecture at U of I. His many building models, put together in long, late-night sessions, usually included long-stemmed dried *Achillea* flower clusters, standing in for trees in his scaled-down, miniaturized designs.

Reading about the ancient medicinal usage of this genus cemented a need in my mind for this herb to be celebrated as an Herb of the Year. If it could be used to staunch blood flow in the Trojan War, why not look at it in detail to see what else had been forgotten in the interim years? To this end, I championed its choice to be among the herbs selected by the International Herb Association, parrying with those who would prefer that mainstream herbs be chosen which might yield a book that would sell well. Many of those well-known herbs have been included as HOYs in recent years, but there is a need to climb that steep learning curve once in a while. The uniqueness of an *Achillea* book might even surprise both readers and writers alike, but even if it doesn't, it will keep the original concept alive.

Achillea filipendulina. Gail Wood Miller

Bios for Illustrators and Photographers

Susan Belsinger—see bio on page 11

Heather Cohen is a freelance graphic artist and web designer. She owns Small House Farm, a sustainable herb farm and seed sanctuary in Michigan. www.Smallhousefarm.com

Gert Coleman—see bio on page 62

Janice Cox — see bio on page 142

Pat Crocker — see bio on page 105

Karen England—see bio on page 119

Pat Kenny — see bio on page 87

Alicia Mann is a classically trained artist and metalsmith at Heritage Metalworks, LTD, in Downington, Pennsylvania. A graduate of Maryland Institute College of Art, she integrates her interests in art and horticulture by growing flowers, herbs, vegetables, and fruit trees. ammann1212@gmail.com

Marge Powell— see bio on page 47

Skye Suter broadcasts her fondness for art and plants through several disciplines. As a writer and illustrator, she contributes to the International Herb Association's annual *Herb of the Year* ™ publication and other freelance projects. Visit Skye's website anherballeaf.com to view her publications, *An Herbal Leaf Journal,* and *An Herbal Leaf Monthly Message*–newsletters which reflect an interest in "plants, nature, art, crafting, cooking, and especially herbs." anherballeaf@gmail.com

Gail Wood Miller is a member of the Musconetcong Watercolor Group and of the Garden State Watercolor Society. Drawing and painting have been hobbies since childhood. Her day job is health and education coach and consultant, focusing on women and children. A retired professor of English and English education, she also speaks and writes about individual learning styles.

Tina Marie Wilcox — see bio on page 27

Cover, Illustration, and Photo Credits

Front Cover:

Background image: Heather Cohen

Back Cover:

Left: Susan Belsinger

Middle: Karen England

Right: Susan Belsinger

Section Covers:

Yarrow monoprints: Susan Belsinger

Page Credits:

p. 12: *Achillea* 'Coronation Gold' at Rosenberry Garden, Maryland. *Susan Belsinger*

p. 58: The Golden Yarrow Fairy. *Alicia Mann*

p. 81: Haiku illustration by *Pat Kenny*

p. 135: Yarrow layed on table. *Heather Cohen*

p. 143: Yellow Yarrow Girl. *Janice Cox*

p. 200: Toronto Botanical Garden, Canada. *Pat Kenny*

Celebrating 30 Years
of Herb of the Year™!

How the Herb of the Year™ is Selected

Every year since 1995, the International Herb Association has chosen an Herb of the Year™ to highlight. The Horticultural Committee evaluates possible choices based on their being outstanding in at least two of the three major categories: medicinal, culinary, or decorative. Many other herb organizations support the herb of the year selection and we work together to educate the public about these herbs during the year.

Herbs of the Year™: Past, Present and Future

1995	Fennel	2011	Horseradish
1996	Monarda	2012	Rose
1997	Thyme	2013	Elderberry
1998	Mint	2014	Artemisia
1999	Lavender	2015	Savory
2000	Rosemary	2016	Capsicum
2001	Sage	2017	Cilantro & Coriander
2002	Echinacea	2018	Humulus
2003	Basil	2019	Agastache
2004	Garlic	2020	Rubus
2005	Oregano & Marjoram	2021	Parsley
2006	Scented Geraniums	2022	Viola
2007	Lemon Balm	2023	Ginger
2008	Calendula	2024	Yarrow
2009	Bay Laurel	2025	Chamomile
2010	Dill		

Books available on www.iherb.org

Join the IHA

Associate with other herb businesses and like-minded folks, network and have fun while you are doing it!

Membership Levels:
$50 Individual Professional
$50 Affiliate Professional
$50 Post Secondary Student
Log onto www.iherb.org to see what we are all about!

Membership includes:
Your business information listed on www.iherb.org
Membership directory
Herb of the Year™ publication
Quarterly newsletters
Online herbal support
Discounts on conference fees
Promotional support for IHA's Herb of the Year program and
    National Herb Week
Support for National Herb Day
Assocation with a network of diverse herbal businesses

www.ingramcontent.com/pod-product-compliance
Lightning Source LLC
Chambersburg PA
CBHW062132020426
42335CB00013B/1184